GW00670547

MACHINE AND HAND KNITTING

Kathleen Kinder

Machine and Hand Knitting:
Pattern Design

B. T. Batsford Ltd, London

ISBN 0 7134 5916 6

Typeset by Servis Filmsetting Ltd. Manchester
and printed by The Bath Press, Bath
for the publishers
B. T. Batsford Ltd
4 Fitzhardinge Street
London W1H 0AH

PICTURE CREDITS

The publishers and author wish to thank the following people and organizations for giving their permission to reproduce the listed photographs and illustrations:

Aisin UK (Fig 2)
BT Batsford Ltd (Figs 47, 81, 97, 123)
Bond Ltd (Fig 142)
Lois Franklin (Fig 110)
Clarice Garnett (Fig 64, 65)
Keiko Hiwatashi (Figs 8, 9, 41, 67, 146)
Alan King (Fig 13)
Knitmaster Ltd (Figs 40, 51, 61, 102)
Knitting International (Figs 15, 26, 50, 140)
Susanna Lewis (Fig 37)
Museum of London (Fig 77)
Museum of North Craven Life (Figs 13, 18)
Nihon Vogue (Figs 38, 42, 44, 45, 112, 115, 132)
Passap, Switzerland (Figs 34, 39)
Patons and Baldwins (Figs 35, 84, 85, 92, 108b, 122)
Platt Hall Gallery of English Costume (Figs 14, 31)
Alex Rowlands (Fig 98)
Shetland Museum (Fig 82)
Slipknot (Fig 17)
The Trustees of the Victoria and Albert Museum (Fig 83)
Welsh Folk Museum (Fig 12)
Whitby Literary and Philosophical Society (Figs 19, 79)
Whitworth Art Gallery (Fig 36)
York Castle Museum (Figs 1, 3, 25, 62, 91, 138, 139)

To celebrate 400 years of hand knitting in the Yorkshire dales (1590) and 400 years of machine knitting in the East Midlands (1589)

CONTENTS

ACKNOWLEDGEMENT

My grateful thanks to the following for all the help so kindly given to me in the preparation of this book:

Aisin (U. K.); Susan Berke; Helen Bonney; Bogod (Passap): Margaret Deshmane; Fashion and Craft; Lois Franklin; Clarice Garnett; Gawthorpe Hall; Doris Harrison; Keiko Hiwatashi; Jones and Brother; Alan King; Knitmaster; Knitting International; Sue Leighton-White; Susanna Lewis; The Museum of London; Ambery Longbottom; Nihon Vogue; The Museum of North Craven Life, Settle; Patons and Baldwins; Platt Hall Gallery of English Costume, Manchester; Profitable Machine Knitting; Margaret Rhodes; Rowan Yarns; Alex Rowlands; The Shetland Museum, Lerwick; Slip-Knot; Pam Turbett; The Welsh Folk Museum, St Fagan's; Whitby Literary and Philosophical Society; Whitworth Art Gallery, University of Manchester; V. and A. Museum, London; York Castle Museum.

A special word of thanks to Richard Rutt, Bishop of Leicester, whose book *A History of Handknitting*, has been an inspiration and an invaluable source of reference. Also, to members of my family – Helen for modelling so willingly in wind and in calm and George, as always, for the photography and typing the script.

INTRODUCTION

I come from a line of Welsh and Scottish hand knitters. My mother knitted for her family and taught both her daughters, while a maiden aunt knitted compulsively and incessantly during every minute of her frequent holidays with us. Then in 1960, the year of our marriage, my husband and I moved to the Yorkshire Dales, home of England's longest knitting tradition. The place where we live has been associated with wool and sheep for many hundreds of years. During the eighteenth century, there was a flourishing hand-knitting industry here and merchants of the staple used to meet in local inns to grade the wool and fix its price. It is not surprising, therefore, with the ghosts of the past all around and an indefinable 'something' in the air, that I returned to knitting again. Only this time I bought a knitting machine and became completely addicted as many have before and since.

Machine knitting, strange as it may seem to those who have been brought up to believe that only hand knitting has a history, is also a tradition in the Dales, as it is in many other places in the UK. I am also a Methodist and Methodism and machine knitting have maintained an unbroken relationship from the eighteenth century. Gravenor Henson, the framework knitters' historian, and James Foster, the Victorian importer and modifier of the Lamb domestic machine, were Methodists, as are two machine-knitting magazine editors of today. In 1952, I was received 'on note' as a Methodist local preacher in Ruddington Methodist Chapel, Nottingham, and did not realise until 25 years later that the event had taken place in a church where framework knitters had worshipped for 200 years.

In 1978, I was among the first to join the newly formed Knitting and Crochet Guild. Largely through contact with some of the most expert and talented hand knitters in this country, my interest in the practice of hand knitting revived. A few years ago, I began to design and hand knit articles again, taking hand knitting into my system as well as machine knitting, though the latter has remained the predominant interest. I have been aware most recently of the emergence of a third group, who enjoy both hand and machine knitting and who do not wish to set the one against the other. This group appears to be swelling in numbers as the craft of hand knitting declines at popular level.

This book then, is by a machine knitter who hand knits and that at least makes a change. Much historical information is included which normally does not apply to hand knitting alone. The history of both crafts is presented as a knit-woven tapestry so that for the first time we can see the strands intermingle and become part of the whole. I have not avoided controversy. My aim is to stimulate thought and discussion concerning which path we should take. I have no doubt at all that it should be the Japanese way of personalized design, pattern-making and presentation. Apart from any other consideration, I see it as the only means to release in all its fullness the creativity that is in everyone.

ONE

A common system

In 1872 Japan entered into Western-style industrialization. Before that she had no indigenous knitting culture and her people had no oral communication of knitting patterns from one generation to the next. Neither did they know what it was like to measure by eye or hand or how to make an intuitive guess at length and breadth according to traditional Western methods. This tradition has been much romanticized by British and American writers on hand knitting, but without a doubt it is now proving to be the greatest stumbling block towards ensuring that knitting skills will continue to be taught. As far as hand knitting is concerned, the West is in the situation where communal communication has gone. What is left are only written versions of oral patterns, conveyed in a no-diagram, abbreviated code, incomprehensible to would-be knitters, and completely at odds with the media communication methods of today. The only exceptions to the rule are the charted patterns provided for jacquard and intarsia designs.

Because of geographical position and the language barrier, Japan's knitting traditions have developed in isolation. Nevertheless, in Japan as in Britain and the USA, hand and machine knitting were industries which made their contribution to the economy before they became leisure pursuits as well. Japan, of course, missed out on the drawing-room boom in needlecrafts which took place in Europe and North America during the nineteenth century. In Britain, the knitting for money aspect of drawing-room knitting has been underemphasized by historians. It is not always easy therefore to make a strict separation between the two types of knitting. Even today, bespoke knitting by hand or

by domestic machine makes an important contribution to the income of many a knit shop.

During the last quarter of the nineteenth century redundant knitting frames and machines, their manuals and Victorian hand-knitting books found their way to Japan, and her people made of them what they could. In the *Knitters' Circular and Monthly Record* (June 1895), published in Leicester for the knitting industry, we are told that the first knitting machines were taken to Japan from England and then from other countries as well. At this period there was little difference between knitting machines for domestic and industrial use except the power to drive them and the environment in which they were used. In the Osaka region in 1895, the machines 'were of hand power and operated in private houses, from one to five being found in a house'.

The view that 'the Japanese have copied all, thus deteriorating it', is certainly not valid now. As far as the knitting crafts are concerned, the Japanese are leaders of innovation. The revival of popular knitting, its continuing growth, the development of a personalized approach and the dissemination of design ideas internationally, could all depend on the acceptance of the Japanese method of approach.

In 1867, the idea that the knitting machine could be adaped for ladies' work in the home was put forward by William Felkin in *The History of the Machine-wrought Hosiery and Lace Manufactures* (1867, reprinted David and Charles 1967). Early in the 1860s, a knitting frame for domestic use had been on show in an exhibition in Cologne. However, knitting with a machine did not accord with the Victorian image of what a lady's pursuits ought

Fig 1
Regency and Victorian pin balls

to be. Ladies, by and large, were not expected to be involved with anything as demeaning as a mechanical device. In spite of that, a few intriguing references to domestic machine knitting occur in needlecraft literature from the late 1870s onwards. Women tutors were employed to teach prospective customers how to use the machines. Two letters in the archives of Jaeger (William Spence Huntly Ltd) show that a Miss Harrison was employed by her own family firm as a tutor in 1878. From a Harrison manual of *c.* 1890, we learn that a Miss Warren, who was blind, could teach anyone similarly handicapped how to use a knitting machine, in her case a circular sock machine. By the end of the nineteenth century, the idea that knitting machines could be employed in the home by a woman was generally accepted but it is very difficult to estimate how many were actually used in this way.

By 1875 or so the demand for machine-knitted goods was centred on accessories like table cloths and shawls, underwear and stockings, until the sports boom of the 1880s onwards which promoted knitted outergarments. The knitting fac-

Fig 2
Socks knitted using a knitting stick or sheath

Fig 3
Miss Warren Harrison's blind tutor (c.1890)

tories that arose were therefore small in comparison with those manufacturing woven cloth.

According to Japanese authorities it was not until 1924 that a lady called Masako Hagiwara, 'invented the first hand knitting machine for the home'. This seems an extraordinary claim when one considers previous developments in the West but the Hagiwara device was completely different from its predecessors in Europe and America. It appears to have been a simple, straight bar frame similar to the one which, it is believed, William Lee made as his prototype for the stocking frame in the 1580s. Certainly the Hagiwara machine was based on a concept of home machine knitting which owed very little to the Victorian hand machine. The latter was essentially an industrial design. The

Japanese saw from the beginning that knitting machines had to be light and easy to use. They had to be attractive in appearance and occupy a space in the modern home no larger than that required by an ironing board. The machines should pack up and be stored easily. Most important of all, the Japanese were the first to see the home knitting machine as the creator of exclusive knitted fashion. There is no doubt that the modern Japanese machine can trace its ancestry back to the Hagiwara device, but nevertheless, in the development towards greater sophistication, Japanese technology has drawn heavily on European tradition and expertise.

When Japanese machines first made their appearance in the West in the 1960s, a comparison was immediately drawn between them and similar products from European firms, products which were much closer to their industrial counterparts. Even today, machine knitters who use both European and Japanese machines recognize a difference in attitude to the operator. The Japanese positively encourage individual creativity and have developed a liberal, imaginative approach to the teaching of personalized design.

One effect of isolation from the West was that Japan escaped the centuries' old antagonism between the two knitting crafts. Modern research has shown that although framework knitting in the seventeenth century did damage the hand knitter's livelihood in Britain, by the eighteenth century framework knitting had different products and therefore different markets. The frames that were smashed in the Luddite riots early in the nineteenth century were destroyed by those framework knitters who 'handframed', or shaped the fabric by hand at their machines. In effect the framework knitters who practised the quicker cut-and-sew methods, undermined the livelihood of all other framework knitters. The new technology of the later nineteenth century eventually destroyed the livelihood of them all. However, hand knitting for money continued long after the handframe had gone into decline though a number of hand and power frames continued well into the twentieth century manufacturing specialized goods like shawls. It is easy to forget that the frame was a pre-Industrial Revolution invention, and hand knitters who still bear a grudge for supposed harm to their historic tradition should study the facts.

Among other arguments used against the machine knitter, there is the belief held by many expert hand knitters that machine knitting is not a craft, and that at best it is a speeded-up version of a poor sort of hand knitting. Critics say that a craft must involve the direct handling of raw materials and that the hand must be intimately involved with the production of the fabric. By implication, therefore, a hand knitter who follows a pattern blindly belongs to a higher order of humanity than a machine knitter who is responsible for the total design and production processes from start to finish. However, there is increasing recognition that the products of hand and standard machine knitting are often complementary and should not

be placed against each other, especially when modern hand knitters refuse to knit with yarn thinner than double knitting in an age when most people have some form of central heating in their homes. In Britain, in a climate which is producing milder winters, I believe more attention should be paid to finer, handcrafted knits.

Other arguments used against machine knitting include one saying that the fabrics it produces are too smooth and therefore have no character. Ironically, when one hand knits in the traditional way in the round using a Shetland knitting pad, or a knitting sheath (stick) as I sometimes do, the fabric that results is surprisingly smooth and even. The stitch and row gauge of my knitted stockings is 32 stitches and 44 rows per 10 cm (4 ins), and is identical with that produced on a standard machine. In fact it is difficult to tell the difference in the fabric. As the Shetlanders know, a woolly horse for

Fig 4
Shetland pad and steel needles for sweater knitting

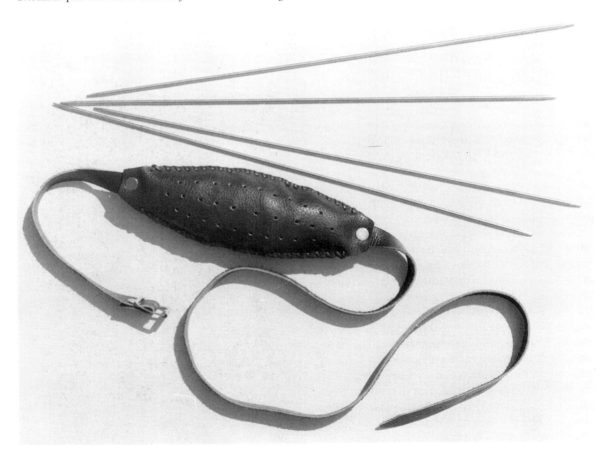

14

Fig 5
Shetland woolly horse for stretching a sweater to size

stretching and blocking woollen garments is the best evener-out of knitted fabrics by hand or by machine. Indeed it is sometimes difficult to tell which part of a Shetland garment has been knitted by which method.

It is the method of knitting and purling unskilfully with needles and yarn held in an inefficient way which produces uneven fabric. Working with several colours across a row in hand knitted Fair Isle or jacquard has a similar effect. What, therefore, is 'interesting' to some is in fact, the product of bad workmanship. While the technique may present an exciting visual appearance, as a wearing fabric it can be board-like and impractical. Provided that a machine knitter has the necessary artistic and technical skills, a surface pattern, machine knitted in two colours, may have greater realism and pictorial qualities than the same pattern hand knitted. Another argument against machine knitting is that it kills colour. There are plenty of hand knitters who do that. Certainly if a machine knitter does not plan colour

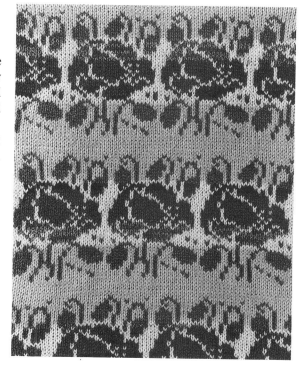

Fig 6
'Poppies' (The Art of Motif-Knitting, *Kinder*)

15

and yarn changes carefully there can be a deadening effect, but it is the knitter who is at fault, not the machine (see Chapter 7).

For those of us who enjoy using knitting needles, hand knitting is a calming therapy, though there are thought-provoking aspects which have been underemphasized in the past. The pleasures of handling the yarn and creating the stitches offset the time factor involved. Moreover, hand knitting can be picked up at any time and in circumstances where one could not operate a machine. Machine knitters, however, have the advantage of speed in the production of most – but not all – fabrics. The craft of handtooling is a craft in its own right.

Hobby machine knitters do not seek speed for the sake of accomplishment, though those who earn money by their craft justifiably do so. Consider the frustration of having so many design projects in the mind and no time to realize them. Machine knitting gives people the opportunity to be creative and

Fig 7

A frame-knitted lace stole

produce results in the time allowed, and that in itself is a boon. Moreover, there are many people who have increased leisure and they don't just want a sedentary unvaried occupation like hand knitting all of the time. They require the stimulus, recreation and challenge presented by a machine, often quite a sophisticated one. Mechanical, technical and electronic expertise and mastery are just as important to many people as handling yarn or a pair of knitting needles and are not to be despised as non-craft activities. These interests should be allowed, especially when beautiful fabrics and personalized quality garments are the result. Design is perhaps just as important as craft in this context. One reason why there are more people (men as well as women) who both hand and machine knit today is due to the fact that people are finding time in their lives for two kinds of knitting activity. This development is the most hopeful yet for future co-operation.

Though the Japanese have not had to agonize over the problems that beset the West, there appear to be others which are theirs alone, and which are to do with the position of women in Japanese society. In 1985, when the slump in the popularity of standard machine knitting in Japan drew comment from writers in the West, Japanese women visitors to English-speaking countries were giving their reasons for the demise of machine knitting and for the popularity of hand knitting in Japan. It was, they said, demeaning and 'not nice' for a woman to use a machine. Japanese men preferred handmade favours from their women as a more sincere sign of affection. Since 1985, however, machine knitting on mostly basic chunky machines has revived; and the relationship with hand knitting has never been closer. There is no coned yarn industry in Japan, and balled yarns are used by both hand and machine knitters. Moreover, the language of communication is identical. At the time of writing, standard gauge machines are coming back into popularity.

Since the Second World War, Japan has been free to develop a logical, mathematical approach to pattern making, an approach which was never the way for just a few gifted designers, but which was and is available for all knitters – hand and machine alike – to understand and develop for themselves.

Fig 8
Keiko Hiwatashi, principal of a Tokyo knitting school. Note her outfit, knitted in Japanese 'summer' yarn

There are knitting schools in Japan where retailers, hobbyists and professional knitters can go for hand- as well as for machine knitting instruction. By presenting a common graphic system for stitch patterns, garment blocks and technical information, Japan has come upon the most effective means of knitting communication for a world conditioned by television, videos and the information revolution by computer. The emphasis is on speed of communication. There is no time to wait for pattern writers to produce patterns in six sizes,

and in any case, the Japanese knitter would feel insulted by the implication that she could not work out her own size from the information given. By employing a universal system of graphics, essential information is communicated to non-Japanese readers. Sophisticated garment designs which would be avoided by designers in the West can be presented in the knowledge that the knitters will understand what is required.

The system took several years to work out. In 1967, the Japanese Industrial Standards Committee finally laid down the format to which all publishing houses concerned with hand and machine knitting publications in Japan now subscribe. This system includes diagrams for patterns, a number code for shaping breakdowns and symbols for stitch patterns, all of which machine knitters everywhere automatically and unknowingly acquire as soon as they buy a Japanese knitting machine and its associated literature in Japanese and English. Sadly, as long as machine and hand knitters elsewhere are kept firmly apart, their respective pattern traditions will continue in isolation. However, some European and American hand knitting authorities have adopted not only garment diagrams but the Japanese symbol system, although the Americans still use Imperial measures. The Japanese symbol system is now regarded as international and in many areas outside Britain there is beginning to be a consensus of opinion that hand and machine knitting ought to have a common pattern format.

The British hand-knit yarn spinners, who are responsible for most of the pattern literature, do not share the enthusiasm for a common system. Since there are a growing number of people who hand and machine knit, and since an increasing number of needlecraft publications are including machine knitting topics in their pages, it seems quite extraordinary to ignore the current 'situation. Hand and machine knitters share a common approach to garment design, yet it is becoming obvious that conflicting advice is being offered to people engaged in both knitting crafts.

Recently a study of education in schools has been done to compare the Japanese attitudes with those in Britain and the USA. The conclusion reached is that greater success comes to Japanese children because they are expected to achieve. When a low ceiling is put on human endeavour, people rarely rise above what is expected. There is an interesting parallel in hand knitting. Although the status of British women in society is considerably higher than that of their counterparts in Japan, in the field of knitting the reverse is true. The British are expected to be obedient and unthinking copy knitters. They are conditioned to dislike diagrams. As a result, knitting in Britain is a craft discipline, whereas in Japan it is both a design and craft discipline. Japanese knitters are expected not only to understand how patterns are put together and work out, but how to make up their own as well. In Britain those functions are appropriated almost entirely by designers and pattern writers.

At present, people are wondering why hand knitting throughout Europe and the USA is suffering such a dramatic decline as a popular craft. Many are expecting machine knitting to follow suit. One could offer many reasons for the decline: high cost of balled yarns, sociological and economic factors, and others to do with fashion and changing leisure patterns, but no one, to my knowledge, has given as a reason the underlying philosophy of the knitter as mere artisan/consumer of branded yarn. Maybe many younger women are unconsciously rebelling against being regarded in this way. Hand knitting is very much a male-dominated industry, with the consumers, mainly women, having little or no say in the direction it should take. In this respect machine knitting is very different. A strong working relationship has developed between the coned yarn producers and the consumers, many of whom are in clubs and classes, and who are not slow in making their requests known. Machine knitting is, of course, a smaller industry than hand knitting.

Great store is now being laid on the teaching of knitting in schools by the yarn spinners, but they cannot expect hand knitting to be taken seriously by education authorities until it is presented as both a design and a craft discipline. One positive aspect of British education is that a high priority is given to developing creativity in children. Merely teaching children how to knit and follow branded patterns is not enough, and quite rightly many teachers refuse to consider hand knitting on those terms. If, however, we were to follow the example of the Japanese, then hand knitting could be presented in a similar way to machine knitting. Links could be made with practical mathematics as well as with art and home economics. A whole structured teaching package could be worked out similar to the one for machine knitting for adults recently published by the City and Guilds of London Institute. For over 30 years there have been classes in machine knitting available in Adult Education colleges in various parts of Britain and, at the time of writing, well over 50 have indicated their willingness to train candidates for the new City and Guilds examination. It is good news that the City and Guilds are interested in developing courses in hand knitting and crochet. One would hope, however, that there could be agreement on design and pattern presentation for crochet and the two knitting crafts.

One of the most disturbing aspects of the modern hand-knit pattern scene is the advice offered on personalized design in the few technical manuals by British authors. Most books on hand knitting, with a few notable exceptions, are glossy books of patterns which do not aim to offer advice on design. In the manuals the 'design your own garment' advice is often nearly 50 years out of date, and so unrelated to modern developments that it is scarcely credible that those responsible should be so unaware of what is happening in the international scene. Why, for example, do hand knit authors continue to advise that every single personalized pattern should be plotted out full scale on mini-gridded graph paper (usually in the wrong proportions)? It is understood that intarsia, fitted sleeve caps, necklines on the bias and special placement patterns have to be planned in this way, but when one is doing, for example, a moss stitch variant on a dropped shoulder line top, why can't a mini-sketch suffice? This is but one topic I deal with in this book (see Chapter 3). Others concern interesting garment shapes, like those with yokes (Chapter 9) or those with bias knitting (Chapter 10), which we don't often see in British hand and machine knit publications. By the old methods, these patterns are difficult to design and pattern write: no wonder we avoid them.

There is a long and rich tradition of

improvization in hand knitting, and there is a valid objection to following a system too rigidly on every occasion. A complicated stitch or surface pattern will inevitably be used with a simple garment shape, lending itself to a choice of increase and decrease placements. The same side of fabric always faces the machine knitter, whereas a hand knitter often has knit and purl rows to consider for pattern breakdowns. Many modern hand knitters organize breakdowns to fall on knit rows only. In this situation they are not following the line of the drawn shape, which is the basic principle of Japanese pattern making. In a simple shape, however, where the line is not critical, surely some choice must be allowed. The Japanese system is most valuable to the knitter who regards the

creative process as beginning from the drawn lines of the garment shape and who regards the structural components as essential parts of the total design. The indications are that the hand knit protagonists of the modern Knitwear Revolution regard the knitted shape as the least important element of a design. Its function is to be the loosely fitting canvas for bold, dramatic and colourful surface patterns. While that movement is still very strong in hand and machine knitting circles, the indications are that today's younger designers, many of whom are involved in both knitting crafts, want to regard structure as a crucial component of garment design. They are also more interested in high standards of technical accomplishment than their predecessors were. The totality makes the impact. If that is so, then the Japanese approach is the one viable alternative to the present confusion.

The Japanese system has little to offer the talented hand knitter who likes to change his or her

Fig 9

A student at Keiko Hiwatashi's knitting school using a ribber

19

mind as the knitting proceeds. This approach is not easy to communicate to others, simply because it depends on an innate ability and an unerring instinct which cannot be articulated. Common advice from a genius is, 'just knit and let the ideas flow'. Sometimes there is a pretence that no maths is involved, and women knitters in particular don't like to own up to using basic mathematical calculations in their knitting, whether intuitively or consciously. Japanese women, who use calculators, computers and all kinds of gadget aids in their knitting design, find Western reluctance to use elementary maths extraordinary. In the same way, they cannot understand the British knitter who likes to be handed a pattern to follow slavishly. As Keiko Hiwatashi explained to a British seminar in 1983, preliminary design and preparation are just as interesting to the Japanese as the actual knitting. If, however, we want hand knitting to recover its importance as a popular handicraft, then we must allow for the availability of a more structured approach, whatever our own habits and attitudes. It is unwise to pour scorn on those who seek to rationalize and organize the means by which creativity can be understood and developed in a practical way.

My years of teaching machine knitting have convinced me that, no matter how inspiring one's lessons are, it is infinitely better to have a system to offer. Not only is continuity ensured, but the rules can be broken as talent reveals itself and confidence grows. Those who do not have exceptional gifts will at least be equipped to attempt projects at the top of their range. If students are not supported by regular teaching and exchange, and readers by a manual to which they can refer, then enthusiasm and inspiration can all too often have the permanence of a soap bubble.

It would, however, be wrong to give the impression that most hand knitters are unthinking copy knitters. There are those who are challenging the status quo within the ranks of their own craft. Well-loved techniques and habits are being questioned, and new avenues of design and stitchcraft are being explored. It would be equally misleading to think that hand knitting cannot be as intellectually challenging and stimulating as machine knitting. The men who are coming into both hand and machine knitting certainly have a different and very refreshing approach. Hand and machine knitters are being invited to put prejudices behind them and seek a common way.

The last few years have seen a growth of interest in historical research. In the past, hand and machine knitters have not been noted for objective and thorough investigation of their inheritance, neither have they known how to use it creatively. Too many hand knitters refuse to look at machine knitting literature, believing that it has nothing to do with them. Too many machine knitters write to magazines with discoveries they claim to have made themselves, which indeed they may have done, but in many cases, though not in all by any means, the discoveries have been recorded in books which the knitters have not read. In this situation we go round in circles and cannot seem to progress beyond what has already been given and received. In my own case, I am puzzled that hand knitters have only recently found the 'ancient' story of Aran knitting to be a fake, when I published the facts as long ago as 1980 (see *A Second Resource Book for Machine Knitters*). In the USA there is the curious case of Virginia Woods Bellamy, who in 1952 patented a method of dealing with bias knitting in garter stitch as her very own invention. Very few modern American hand knitters appear to have heard of her, yet bias knitting in garter stitch is very popular in the USA and a number of patterns have been published (see Chapter 10).

The time has come to urge people to delve into the background, not only to check whether what they have discovered has been done before and to give credit where credit is due, but also to reveal the riches that the past can offer. Moreover, hand and machine knitters should co-ordinate their efforts in historical study. In the Knitting and Crochet Guild we are finding that research done in isolation can make fools of us all.

One way to stimulate growth and interest in the knitting crafts is to have an absorbing new design approach and to give consideration to the totality of all the elements which go to make a garment that is a pleasure to wear or a hanging that is a delight to behold. Each ought to be regarded as an art form in its own right. The design preparation is in itself an intriguing activity. There are all kinds of facets –

technical, sartorial and aesthetic – to explore. Crafts have to move on and develop. If they stand still and cease to be meaningful, then they become a subject for history alone and not for current practice. Though hand and machine knitters are delighted by the public's interest in the history of their craft, one feels that often the interest is based on nostalgia and a mistaken view of what knitting was like in days gone by. James Norbury was Patons' famous hand knitting consultant in the 1950s and '60s. He wrote a remarkably prophetic chapter on the home knitting machine in Odham's *Encyclopaedia of Knitting* (1961), but his words have wider application for us now: 'This attitude of looking backwards to a land of promise has always been a fool's paradise'.

If there is considerable historical content in this book, it is because I look not backwards but forwards to a land of promise in which knowledge of our history helps us to understand where we are now and which way we must go. We are recovering a true historical perspective in the study of hand and machine knitting history. We now look with disfavour on those who distort historical facts in order to give an advantageous commercial slant. Instead we see that the facts of history relating to both machine and hand knitting, and presented as truthfully as our present knowledge will allow, are fascinating in themselves. The study of history must, however, go alongside the practice of our craft. Once history becomes more important than practice, the knitting craft can only end up as a museum piece, its activity, practice and creativity frozen in yesterday.

TWO

Communication: oral to written

The dissolution of the monasteries in the reign of Henry VIII and the tremendous social upheaval it caused in rural England is often given as one reason why there were so many rootless poor in the latter half of the sixteenth century. In my part of the Yorkshire Dales the land and property belonged to four great abbeys, of which Fountains was the most important. Abbey retainers, their shepherds and servants, found that they had no legal rights whatsoever and many were left dispossessed and homeless when the abbeys' properties were confiscated and sold to private individuals.

The reign of Elizabeth I was a more settled time and there was a small increase in population, barely diminished by several outbreaks of plague. One particularly severe one was in 1597, the date on the plague stone in the village where I live.

Queen Elizabeth established the Poor Law, which forced urban and rural communities to make provision for the poor and unemployed, and knitting schools featured largely amongst the success stories brought about by the requirements. There are quite a few references in county and town records throughout England to the setting up of knitting institutions. From the very first the communication of knitting skills had to be by oral explanation accompanied by the study of knitted items. Such is the nature of knitted fabric that it is relatively easy to formulate a recipe from close examination of the stitches, rows and shaping breakdowns. Any knitter who is reasonably expert and who can count can easily tell others what to do. In Richard Rutt's *History of Handknitting* (Batsford 1987) there is an interesting quotation from Edmund Howes' *Annals* (1615), in which Howes describes how in 1567 an apprentice called

William Rider borrowed a pair of knit worsted stockings in the lodging of an Italian merchant, 'and caused other stockings to be made by them, and these were the first worsted stockings made in England'. If that is so, then that must also be the first recorded example of plagiarism in knitwear.

It is interesting that most of the knitting schools mentioned in records, in particular York, Lincoln and Norwich, were on the eastern side of England, though indeed the Midlands, parts of Dorset, Hampshire and Gloucester were also famous for stocking knitting from the last half of the sixteenth century onwards. Stocking knitting is mentioned in the Shetlands as early as 1615. The counties of the eastern seaboard were where Flemish refugees first settled, and they brought with them considerable textile skills, among which was an expert knowledge of stocking knitting. One early teacher of knitting, John Cheseman, must have been quite celebrated because he was involved with both the knitting school at Lincoln and the one at York. In Lincoln, Cheseman was bound by his agreement, 'to set to work in his science all such as are willing to come to him . . . and to hide nothing from them that belongeth to the knowledge of the said science'. In other words, stocking knitting was recognized as a skill, and the teacher had to communicate all he knew. It is unlikely that many of his pupils could read.

Hand knitting soon moved out of the more prosperous towns like York, where other trades flourished. In some cases, it was supplanted in the seventeenth century by framework knitting. In the Settle-Giggleswick area of the Yorkshire Dales, the hand-knitting industry lasted until the end of the eighteenth century, when the new Leeds-Kendal

Fig 10
Dalesbred and Rough Fell sheep, Giggleswick

turnpike road brought better communications and alternative employment. Hand knitting continued to flourish in the more remote upper dales. In the Richmond area of North Yorkshire in 1595, only a few years after the York school had been set up, there were a thousand stocking knitters. Improved rods for knitting needles aided the spread of knitting, and so did the newly developed spinning-wheel, which replaced the slower distaff method of the Middle Ages. In the wool-producing areas, the poor had a long-established right to pluck scraps of wool from the fields, fells and hedgerows. In the Giggleswick bylaws of 1564 it is stated 'that none shall gather wooll in the fields before the cattle be all gone forth, nor shall gather wooll on the Scarr before Midsummer in paine of six shillings and eightpence'. In the mid-eighteenth century, the wool gathered from the hedgerows provided one

source of raw material for members of the Trefeca settlement organized by the evangelist Howel Harris in an attempt to remedy the poverty of people in Wales. Of 50 people in the settlement, 36 were women engaged in picking wool, carding flax, spinning and knitting stockings. It is strange that wool-gathering now means absent minded when in the old days it was often all that stood between people and starvation.

In Richmond in 1595, the knitters bought wool from the wool house and could only use it for the purpose of knitting stockings. One spinner could supply several knitters with all the wool they could knit. From early days the Yorkshire Dales industry was organized and structured, and middle men, merchants and hosiers controlled the development from the market down to the spinners and knitters toiling in their homes or outside when they had a moment to spare between labouring jobs for farmers and landlords. In the countryside, knitting was a social activity and no doubt skills were learnt

Fig 11
Cage Farm, Dentdale, home of an eighteenth-century knitting school

simply by watching others. Knitting gatherings were common in many places, partly to economize by using just one light in a cottage and partly for company.

Even though they were established at the end of the sixteenth century, it was still necessary to have knitting schools in the eighteenth century. In Dent there were four, of which Cage Farm was one. In the Hon. Rachel Kay-Shuttleworth's collection at Gawthorpe Hall I found a copy of a Yorkshire Dales dialect poem by A. E. Whitehead, called 'The Turble Knitters of Dent'. The speaker in the poem is obviously a girl who is being prepared to start as a pupil in a knitting school:

Fig 12
A Welsh knitter (c.1880–90)

24

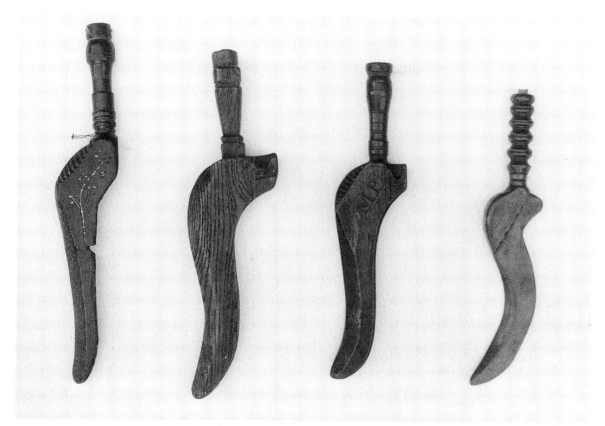

Fig 13
Dales knitting sticks or sheaths

'Mi Mudther gaed me a strang blue band
(waist belt to hold a knitting stick)
Mi Fadther meead me methra pricks (four
needles)
A clue of bump (ball of coarse wool) mi
Grandma wound
I need nowt else to knit at skeul (school).'

Betty Yewdale's classic description of life in an
eighteenth-century Dent knitting school in Robert
Southey's *The Doctor* is well known. Speed was the
aim of the teaching. The pupils all knitted together,
and if they didn't come up to standard they were
'weel thumpt' (well beaten). Betty Yewdale also
gives us a clue that stocking knitting in the Dales
was regarded very much as the employment of the
poor when she tells us that Dent was considered by
the Kendal people to be 'the poorest place in the
world'.

By about 1750, however, knitting was also
appearing alongside other needlecrafts as an activity which could be followed by the middle and
upper classes, though its acceptance as such was
apparently confined to certain areas of the country.
Jane Austen's Hampshire and Hertfordshire hero-
ines (*c.*1810–16) did not knit. In *Pride and Preju-
dice*, when Mr Bingley was called upon to list the
accomplishments of young ladies he said, 'They all
paint tables, cover skreens and net purses'. In
Emma, Miss Bates, the impoverished daughter of a
clergyman, is a knitter. She hovers on the brink of
gentility, but cannot be regarded in the same social
class as Emma herself.

The framework knitters 1600 to 1800

Whatever Gravenor Henson's lack of qualifications
as a professional historian, his *History of the
Framework Knitters* (1831, reprinted David and
Charles, 1970) makes fascinating reading, not

least for the vivid thumbnail sketches he draws of the characters of the framework knitters, their technicians the framesmiths, and the wealthy and better educated hosiers who often tried to cheat the knitters out of their due reward for inventions and discoveries. The authenticity of the description of how William Lee first knitted a stocking on his newly invented frame may be dubious to some, but to a machine knitter who uses a modern single bed machine the description strikes true. According to Henson's sources, William Lee nearly gave up his invention in the 1580s because it seemed impossible to make a machine which knitted a 'round web'. Indeed, it wasn't until 1816 that Sir Marc Isambard Brunel produced a circular frame that could knit seamless tubes of fabric. According to Henson, Lee observed that in hand knitting the knitter turned the heel on two needles: 'the thought struck him instantly that he could make a flat web and them by joining the selvedges with a needle make it round'.

The heel nearly defeated William Lee because there were no holding cams on the handframe. However, the craft of handtooling on the machine began with the manual shaping of a stocking heel, and all parts were seamed up on completion of the knitting. We are left in no doubt that a hand-knitted stocking was the starting point. Thereafter, the framework knitter had to adapt to suit his own medium. What many modern knitters do not realise is that the needles were immovable on the old frame, which was literally a mechanized version of the primitive peg frame. It represented a completely different tradition of knitting from that done by two or four needles. Which of hand knitting and basic frame is the older method, or whether each developed alongside the other, is currently the subject of debate.

The real concern of the framework knitters from the seventeenth century onwards was to see that none of their skill was communicated to foreigners or to fellow countrymen who might be competitors. The knitters did their best to ensure that none of their discoveries and inventions was carried overseas. Since no instructions were in document form, restrictions were placed on people and on their movements. Clause 24 in the London Framework Knitters' Charter (1664) reads, 'The invention being purely English . . . no person, whether freeman or foreigner, denizen or alien, shall presume to carry, or cause to be carried, any frames used for making silk stockings or used in framework knitting beyond the seas, upon any pretence whatsoever.'

Framework knitters within 20 miles of the City of London were commanded to bind their children to be apprentices to the trade for seven years: such were the safeguards taken to avoid plagiarism. In 1776, in Nottingham, there was the celebrated case of Branson, who was alleged to have stolen nine frames which were modified by a device patented by one Morris. Branson escaped on board a ship bound for France, but was pursued and brought back to England. He was fined heavily and forced to work for Morris for the rest of his life. One hundred years after Branson, the prohibition under Clause 24 was completely ignored and forgotten, as redundant frames, knitting machines and manuals were shipped out to Japan. No one gave a thought to the fact that the technology of yesterday could shape the technology of tomorrow in the hands and minds of the innovative and skilful. Had the prohibitions of the Framework Charter been observed, the history of the domestic knitting machine in the twentieth century could have been very different.

Stockings were not the only items knitted on the frame. During the eighteenth century, beautiful lace was also knitted. At first the framework knitters copied from hand knitting, but by 1770 original stitches were being developed, and pieces for waistcoats, shirts and breeches were produced. Space-dyed silks were used, and intarsia knitting was worked manually by the laying-over method which is so popular today. During the eighteenth century, the majority of large framework knitted items were produced for cut-and-sew. In the Gallery of English Costume, Platt Hall, Manchester, there is a most interesting waistcoat which is frame knitted with stripes of variegated silk. The garment is cut-and-sewn and lined. Fully fashioned knitting, apart from stocking shaping, had not yet arrived. One very intriguing reference in Henson's book is to fleecy greatcoats which appear to have been knitted in pile stitch. There is no reference to how they were shaped, although Henson makes it

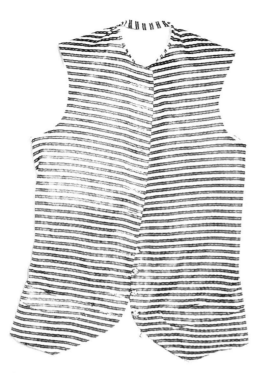

Fig 14
An eighteenth-century frame-knitted waistcoat

clear that these were complete garments and not pieces. The fleecy greatcoats were knitted on frames so huge that two strong men were required to press off the loops and operate the bar. Two such mechanical monsters were known by the names of 'Gog' and 'Magog', after two pagan gods in the Old Testament. 'Gog' stayed in Nottingham with its inventor, the remarkable William Horton, while 'Magog' went to Godalming in Surrey where James Whitehorn, a man of exceptional strength, operated it for 26 years 'unaided and unharmed'.

The first written patterns

In the east Midland villages around Nottingham and Leicester, the framework knitters' lives and ways of earning their living bore similarities to those of their hand knitting counterparts in the Yorkshire and Cumbrian Dales and, indeed, in other parts of the country. Framework knitters lived in community groups in village complexes, and no doubt shared their skills among their families and associates. In the Midland towns, many knitters were employed in small factories, known as frame shops, before the introduction of the larger units.

There is no doubt that as long as people earn money by their knitting skills there is going to be little free-for-all information on techniques and design for the general public. It was as true of the hand and machine knitters of the past as it is of their designer counterparts of today. The oldest extant English knitting pattern, dated 1655, was analysed by Richard Rutt in his *History of Handknitting*. This pattern or recipe was printed in a medical compendium, and one wonders for whom it was intended, since most peasant knitters could not read. The suggestion is that perhaps, even at this point in time, there were educated knitters from the middle or upper classes of society who wanted to knit stockings.

The first reference I can find to written instructions for machine knitters is from Henson's book. In *c.*1750, Charles Villiers, a master stocking knitter who was allegedly a descendant of George Villiers, Duke of Buckingham, favourite of James I and Charles I, wrote out on cards instructions for his knitters on how to improve the narrowing (shaping) of their stockings. Henson said that Villiers did this in spite of its seeming 'vainly ludicrous and puerile'. The suggestion is that information was passed by word of mouth or by observing others, and that no self-respecting knitter ought to have it written down. Significantly, these workmen could read, and this marks a step forward in the progress towards written communication. Helen Bonney, writing in *Slip Knot* (June 1988), the magazine of the Knitting and Crochet Guild, has argued very convincingly that Villiers wrote the pattern in the form of a jingle so that his knitters could memorize the instructions without looking too often at the card.

As late as 1826 in the Yorkshire Dales, Joseph Dover, hosier, wrote to Daniel Dover that the only way for Daniel Dover to find our how to hand knit Kilmarnock caps was 'to have a knitter from these parts'. In other words, there was no other means of communicating the information except by sending one who kept the knowhow in his head and who could interpret it with his hands. The ploy may, of course, have been a safeguard to keep the information away from competitors.

The written recipe for hand-knitting

By 1851, the year of the Great Exhibition, the full effects of the Industrial Revolution were being felt. Throughout the nineteenth century there were sweeping social changes which had a dramatic effect on the lives of women. Middle-class wives of prosperous Victorian industrialists and merchants were expected to reflect the proudly won social status of their husbands, which meant, in the main, remaining at home and doing nothing that was considered degrading. The concept of Woman as Ornament to her husband arose. In 1851, out of a population of about six million women over 20 years of age, one half had no place in non-domestic industry, and stayed at home as wives and daughters. If they remained as spinsters or became widows, they had to depend on private means or on the goodwill of relatives for support.

In all the consideration writers have given to the flowering of knitting and needlecraft in the Victorian era, little has been said about that species of humanity, the 'distressed gentlewoman,' condemned by status not to earn a living in the manner of the lower classes, but having to find some acceptable means of eking out a pittance in her widow- or spinsterhood that would save her from ignominy or starvation, or both. The evidence shows that hand knitting was both a money spinner and a leisure pursuit; hand knitters today who designate hand knitting as a leisure craft and domestic machine knitting as an industry should study the history of both. In any case, a leisure pursuit to the Victorians had to be useful. Enjoyment was a secondary consideration.

Mrs Gaugain has been hailed as one of the pioneer writers on needlecraft, and the preface to the second volume of *The Lady's Assistant for executing useful and fancy designs in Knitting, Netting and Crochet* (1842), leaves us in no doubt that she is not only helping the comfortably-off woman to employ her leisure usefully, but that she, Mrs Gaugain, is doing a service to the distressed gentlewoman and those women of the lower classes who could read. In other words we have a manual for work and leisure containing recipes for items that can be sold, as well as for items to knit for family and home:

'It gives me much pleasure to learn from various quarters that my first effort has been the means of affording a genteel and easy source of livelihood to many well-disposed and industrious females both in the humble and middle ranks of life, and at no period could a work of this kind be more desirable than at present'.

The arrival from Europe of Berlin wool in all its variety of colours gave a real impetus to needlepoint embroidery, knitting and crochet. Mrs Gaugain's instructions for bags, stockings, comforts, tidies and table covers are extremely clear, and she specifies yarn quantities. The patterns are oral instructions written down, but it was to be another 60 to 80 years before we were to see a knitting language and abbreviated code, and before the stitch and row tensions are mentioned.

Throughout the nineteenth century, writers were to emphasize polite ways of holding the needles, and Mrs Gaugain, rather unusually, recommends the German way 'as the more elegant mode to hold the thread over the forefinger of the left hand and not in the right as most people do'. EMC, the author of the *Lady's Knitting Book*, published by Hatchards, London, in 1883, also recommends the German way. She disagrees about its attractive appearance, 'but it is so much quicker when once learnt'. This author advises children to learn to knit by producing bath towels, floor cloths and dishcloths using number 14 pins. For a dishcloth one needs three strips sewn together, and the instructions for one strip are 'knit backwards and forwards on 30 stitches for half a yard, and sew the three strips together'. Such vagueness assumes a degree of proficiency in the reader who perhaps would learn to knit in the old social way and by studying stitch patterns on samplers and items for wearing and decoration.

It is very difficult to assess just how far knitting was regarded as a drawing-room occupation alongside other branches of needlework like embroidery and crochet, which were often given more space in those needlecraft publications devoted to several crafts. Moreover, garments executed in crochet frequently showed more sophisticated techniques of shaping than those done in knitting. One suspects that although knitting was a universal accomplishment, it tended to be taken for granted. In *Needlework* by M. K. Gifford (Nelson, 1913), we read, 'Knitting is so essentially a commonplace industry that it seems natural to picture it as followed from the beginning of time'.

For all the thousands of knitted items produced by the Victorians, the truth was that knitting had not yet come into its own. Its full potential as an apparel medium had yet to be realized.

The arrival of the Victorian domestic machine

The inventions of the latch needle in 1847 by the French and then, around 1862, the domestic V-bed machine by Isaac Lamb, an American Baptist pastor, ushered in a new era of home mechanized knitting. The connected two-bed machine for plain and purl rib knitting may look cumbersome beside our modern machines, but it was a featherweight compared to the frame. James Foster of Preston

Fig 15
James Foster's improved designing machine
(Knitter's Circular and Monthly Record, *September 1898*)

began to import the Lamb machine into England in 1867. His example was soon followed by William Harrison of Manchester, whose brand name was the most well-known of any. Both men had considerable inventive gifts. Modern domestic machine knitters remember James Foster as the inventor of the double-jacquard card system in use on today's Japanese punchcard machines. It is significant that both men were from the north of England, where there was, and still is, more poverty than in the south, and where there was more need for the domestic machine.

Another machine to arrive in Britain at that time was the American Crane Knitter as announced by Cassell's *Household Guide* of 1870. It may have been a Lamb machine by another name. The tension arm resembled 'a well-made trout or salmon rod', and the machine could knit a pair of socks in 25 minutes.

A circular sock machine which arrived in the early 1870s was very popular, and both Foster and Harrison imported that also. In some of Foster's manuals of 1890 it is noted that boys' jerseys were knitted on the circular sock machine, presumably on the half tubular setting. Since there were not sufficient needles for the back/front, each of these was done in two pieces and seamed up the middle. The sock machines were made to earn their keep, and in rural areas like the Yorkshire Dales they, and small V-beds, were very popular (there is a

Fig 16
*A machine-knitted tuck stitch sweater –
date unknown*

small collection of machines in the Upper Dales Folk Museum at Hawes and a much larger one in Bradford Industrial Museum). It would appear that knitting machines were often bought to knit large items like jerseys, jackets and adult undergarments. There were comparatively more patterns, also known as recipes, for these articles in machine pattern books than there were for their equivalent in publications for hand knitting.

Changes in the last half of the nineteenth century

Despite the speed of such machines, they do not seem to have been accepted as fit for a lady to work for some considerable time. The movement towards the emancipation of women, the impact of the Education Acts (1870 onwards) and the sports boom of the last two decades of the century were, however, preparing the way for a change of attitude. The Crimean War of the 1850s had had a profoundly sobering effect. It was the first of the wars in which women contributed to the war effort

Fig 17
*A hand-knitted girl's sweater (*Leach's Penny Knitter, *date unknown)*

by knitting for the men at the front. Even Queen Victoria did her bit in this respect. The death of the Prince Consort in 1861 and a queen who went into mourning and stayed there for the rest of her life also cast a shadow across Victorian society. Frivolity was out of fashion. Many of the hand knitting manuals of the 1870s and 1880s were severely practical and even moralistic in their choice of recipes and advice compared with some of their predecessors.

The 1870s saw the formation of a number of societies through which the distressed gentlewomen might sell their work. By the last quarter of the nineteenth century, their number had increased dramatically. Sad little adverts began to appear in the ladies' and needlecrafts magazines. Among those in an 1871 issue of *The English*

Fig 18
A nineteenth-century domestic V-bed machine

Woman's Magazine was, 'Dora knits (nicely) socks or stockings for ladies, gentlemen or children in any material. Will take orders. Ilfracombe. Devon.'

To Dora and to others like her, the magazine offered little consolation:

> 'We grieve that it is not in our power to assist you. Needlework is a drug in the work market, and even the most successful workers earn little. Thousands of letters such as yours are received by us yearly and we are obliged to own our inability to solve the problem of employment for women.'

Some, like Charlotte Bronte's Jane Eyre, were able to find employment as governesses. Others must have taken to writing, for there was a veritable flood of publications on the needlecrafts by middle- and upper-class women.

Mrs Leach's Fancy Work-Basket (1886)

In my collection I have a bound edition of all the issues of this title for 1886. Since there is considerable hand knitting content in all of these, the publication offers a real insight into the state of the craft in the last quarter of the nineteenth century. First, the black and white illustrations reveal an unequal quality in the knitting designs. Some knitted pieces look quite tatty and badly executed. Others are beautifully even. The polite way of holding the right needle, like a pen, was obviously beginning to have the effect that one can still see today. The advice, too, has a familiar ring. It is advice you do not require if you knit in the old peasant way with the right needle controlled for movement: 'Those who knit loosely might use a size finer needle.'

Those who knit too tightly, it appears, are not considered, but maybe tight knitting was not a problem. Occasionally one is given the length of the garment, but there is no stitch and row gauge: that did not appear until the early years of the twentieth century. Only one size is provided in each pattern. Since measurements are rare, one wonders how the knitters managed. Presumably they would try the pattern as printed then alter the measurements to suit. Instructions are written out in full. The time for abbreviations had not yet arrived. Some instructions are very longwinded. For y.o. we read: 'make a stitch by throwing the wool over the needle'.

Of course, y.o. could not be used until there was a sufficiently large number of people who would know what the abbreviation meant. It takes time for a language of communication to be established. Mrs Leach's pattern writers didn't know how to increase fully fashioned. To increase you are instructed to pick up the stitch bar in the row below or put the thread forward, and of course a hole is the result. Knit 2 together appears more often than passing the slipped stitch over, though k2tog may in some instances mean k2tog tb1 (through back of the loop, which gives a right lean). The asterisk is used to indicate repeats, and in a few patterns one is advised to knit for so many inches per stage of construction.

There are some beautiful stitch patterns in the magazines, especially in lace, and there is a wide variety of garments, some of them showing a remarkable understanding of sophisticated construction methods. For a gentleman's cardigan jacket, using size 16 needles for the rib and 12 for the main part, you cast on 200 stitches for the back and two fronts. The instructions for the pocket slits, armholes, and indeed the whole garment, are extremely clear. Furthermore, the sleevehead is curved slightly by the short row method. There are patterns for mantles, hoods and wraps, but there are no outer garments for ladies. Unexpectedly there are short rows in sideways knitting incorporated in petticoats for children and grown ups, with some pleated effects emphasized by ribbed arrangements. The petticoats are the forerunners of the machine-knitted skirts in the 'total look' fashions of today. There is also the use of waste yarn to hold stitches, known to Mrs Leach as 'coarse wool of any kind'.

Among the more unusual stitches are a form of two-colour Fair Isle in garter stitch, loop stitch and cabling and moss stitch variations reminiscent of gansey knitting. These are done with three needles, two for the knitting and a third used for the cable. Mrs Leach does not share the modern phobia about decreasing on the purl row: 'Decrease at the end of each row, either by knitting 2 together or purling 2 together, whichever agrees with the pattern in each respective row'.

More on the distressed gentlewoman

The correspondence columns make interesting reading, and show that *Mrs Leach's Fancy Work-Basket* was inundated with letters and advertisements from people desperate to sell their work. Mrs Leach gives the addresses of at least 15 societies which can help ladies provide a market place for their work. Her comment is biting and surprisingly feminist:

'It is sad that amongst all the branches of employment that the benefactors of our race profess to have opened out to women, we can still find so few roads open to those who are really gentlewomen both by birth and education, and who yet are forced to seek some means of earning or at least augmenting their income'.

The distress was not only felt by gentlewomen, as defined by the snobbish Mrs Leach, but by those whose family had made it into the new middle-class, and who therefore had a status to maintain. Margaret Deshmane, writing in *Slip Knot* (June 1986), quoted an answer to a correspondent in *The Girl's Own Paper* of 18 August 1883, which strikes a surprisingly modern note:

'We sympathise much with you in your various troubles and are glad to find you so self reliant and brave. With regard to the knitting machine, we think you would find it answered if you could always be sure of getting work for it. This you should enquire about before expending the money'.

Despite all the suffering that was hidden under the needlework boom, the flood of publications rapidly aided the spread of skills among the female population, both the poor and comfortably off. The publications in the main catered for a sophisticated knitting group who would soon be able to cope with abbreviations and tension gauge. The day of the diagram was still a little way off.

The Jersey-Guernsey tradition

One garment in particular illustrates the diverging histories of hand and machine knitting. It is possible to trace fishermen's guernseys, *i.e.* ganseys, right back to the undergarments of the seventeenth century, but ganseys, with cabling and textured patterns, were not really well-known before the middle of the nineteenth century. Knit frocks – a type of jersey – were produced in Cornwall in the first two decades of the century and later in the Yorkshire Dales. Moreover, they were made on handframes as early as 1815. In a letter to Messrs William and John Kynaston, 2 December 1835, Joseph Dover apologizes for the small quantity of knit frocks he is sending because the Yorkshire Dales knitters preferred to knit smaller items like stockings by hand. The shape of the majority of Dales knitting sheaths – or sticks as they are popularly known – with their diagonal resting ledge, favoured stocking and glove knitting. Victorian V-bed machines, however, were eventually introduced to produce the knit frocks and jackets which the hand knitters refused to do by hand. The Cornish sheaths, however, had a long slit enabling them to be moved around the belt more easily. So, in Cornwall, the hand knitters produced ganseys for the trade, while sock machines were brought in to do the stockings. On the Yorkshire coast, too, gansey knitters knitted the garment in the round with five needles, but using a knitting sheath. So much for the destruction of hand knitting by the machine.

The fisherman's gansey has been well documented. The basic dropped shoulder line shape has had a great influence on the modern knitted-top produced by two needles, not four or five. By the end of the nineteenth century the camera was recording some of the images of fishing life, men with their faces full of character, and their womenfolk toilworn, but often knitting when they were not gutting the fish. In museums down the north eastern and eastern seaboard of Scotland and England are magnificent photos of fisherfolk and

Fig 19
Lifeboatman Harry Freeman wearing his gansey

seamen. Because the fisher gansey was the badge of the community at the turn of the century, it was worn by nearly every man. Though the schools with their knitting drills taught a different kind of knitting, the teaching was obviously beneficial. It is interesting that, no doubt as a result of what was taught at school as well as in the home, some beautiful Fair Isle and Shetland colour knitting was also done at the turn of the century.

Two knitting languages

At this time, two knitting languages began to emerge. Clara Sedgwick, one of the last authentic Yorkshire Dales knitters, who died in Settle in 1987, was born in Dentdale in 1898. Her father taught her to knit when she was four, and the yarn used was pulled-back cotton from flour bags. Mrs Sedgwick spoke two knitting languages, that of the

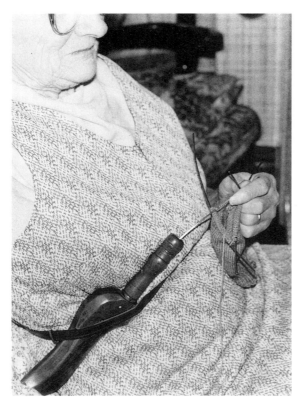

Fig 20
The late Clara Sedgwick demonstrating the use of a knitting stick (1987)

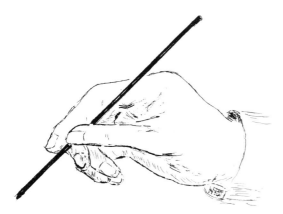

Fig 21
How to hold the right needle the polite way

Dales and that of the elementary school knitting drill. My mother, a Scot, born in the same year, has a similar background. They knitted their stockings in the old way, with four needles, and with the knitting stick in the case of Mrs Sedgwick, and their lace knitting and other modern items with two needles in the 'new' way. Neither, however, took any notice of the teaching to hold the right needle like a pen, and their judgement was sound. My mother and aunt taught me to tuck a long needle under the right arm with the end in the oxster (Scottish for armpit). Today, I prefer to use a circular needle. Mother and her sisters had to knit their own black stockings and always went out to play with their stocking knitting in their hands. They had so many rows to do before they came in for supper, and the place on the stocking was marked with a thread. One of my aunts used to cheat and move the thread to her advantage.

Whatever we think of enforced knitting, of learning to knit by rote, and everyone casting on and knitting together, such training has had a profound effect on the knitting traditions of Britain. That teaching has now worked its way through the generations. There is nothing to take its place and we are the poorer as a result.

The acceptance of the Victorian domestic machine

Towards the end of the nineteenth century, the domestic machine began to be more widely accepted. The conclusion to Mrs E. Lewis's book, *Wools and How to Use Them* (1884), is devoted to the knitting machine:

'It is an admirable invention, perfectly satisfactory in every way, but its present high price prevents its being adopted in ordinary households.

It is very generally used in large institutions; it has already found its way into some English homes, and a case was brought under my notice quite recently of a lady who had made a large sum of money towards building a church from the profits of her knitting machine.'

Obviously in 1884 there was no interest-free credit by which one could buy a machine. The knitting clubs, however, who today run many events in aid of various good causes, have an honourable precedent. What is so interesting about the machine knitting lady in Mrs Lewis's book is that she does not seem to be in the least 'distressed' and can afford to spend her leisure time in making money for charitable purposes. She is, in fact, the kind of person who supports the currently popular view of Victorian needlework as mainly for leisure. The irony is that she was a machine knitter and not a hand knitter. Mrs Lewis concludes, 'If we ever do find ourselves the happy possessor of this delightful invention we shall find our knowledge, skill and experience more valuable every day.'

Mrs Lewis thinks that the knitting machine could be used by 'the better class of servants', but declares prophetically that 'in the next generation, it will be considered quite as much a necessity as the sewing machine is now'. She also leaves us in no doubt that a machine is for the experienced and proficient. Her comment that the machine did not do fancy work is revealing. It did, but not of the kind she recognized. She suggests that machine knitters should learn all they can about knitting, *i.e.* hand, presumably so that they can handtool at the machine. There were in fact instructions for the handtooling of lace and other patterns in most manuals. Mrs Lewis's suggestion at least gives us an indication as to why there were no machine knitting patterns in needlecraft manuals.

There were, however, plenty of knitting-machine adverts aimed at women in the home. In late Victorian times, women were looking for equality, emancipation and universal adult suffrage, and not particularly for ways to use their intelligence and expertise in needlecraft, a symbol to many of domestic subservience. A radical new approach was not to come for a hundred years. There were signs of the tensions that were developing between hand and machine knitters who wanted to earn money. The advice to one correspondent in an issue of *The Girl's Own Paper* (24 April 1883) reads as follows, 'You could never knit or crochet such beautifully fitting jerseys as are now machine made in every colour and in excellent wool. The same may be said of cardigan vests.'

One reason why we hear more of the problem of the distressed gentlewoman in the last 25 years of Victoria's reign is simply because machine-made products were more readily available, and the market for items handmade in the drawing room was disappearing fast.

The Harrison Knitting Machine Manual, No 21

The copy of this manual in my collection, is from between 1890 and 1900. It has been dated by means of a picture in it of a lady wearing a pair of knitted knee-length riding tights, below which peep black stockings decorated with embroidered clox. This fashion was all the rage in the mid-1890s. The manual is very well organized with a series of lessons on how to set up the machine and work the various processes before introducing the knitter to the patterns which are very interesting and varied. Some are new stitches to try on items like scarves, shawls, antimacassars and so on. Most of the stitches cannot be hand knitted as they are swung cardigan or fishermen's rib stitches requiring one of the beds to be racked from side to side. There are also some beautiful stitch arrangements, some of which I have never seen before. Cardigan stitch was popular in the 1950s and 1960s when

Fig 22
A pair of ladies' machine-knitted riding tights (Harrison manual, c.1895)

the Swiss double-bed machines were marketed, and I have revived some examples recently in my *Machine Knitter's Book of the Ribber, Vol 2*. It took a little time to work out the Victorian ones and to understand how the racking system worked on the old machines. Among the garments included are six patterns for ladies' full-length coats, and one for a ladies' two-piece suit. These garments herald the total-look, machine knit fashions of the 1920s and 1980s. The sports boom was in full swing in the 1890s, and adults were wearing knitted outerwear for golf, cycling and riding.

The format of the patterns as they appear in the manual would not be unfamiliar to Mrs Leach. There are no abbreviations and no tension swatches, but we are told exactly which tension number on the dial to use. Taking out and narrowing, the old framework knitting terms for increasing and decreasing, are employed, and where the modern Japanese would convey all by a small diagram, the author of the Harrison manual needs half a page to tell in words how to hold and use the transfer tool. However, the needle arrangements for the double-bed patterns are shown in the way we would show them today. The needle arrangement for a cardigan stitch pattern illus-

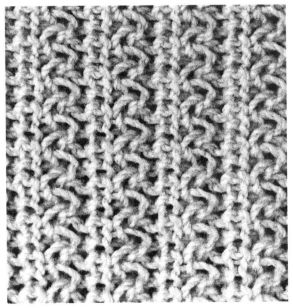

Fig 23
Victorian 'cardigan' stitch for slippers

Fig 24
Examples of Victorian 'cardigan' stitch, knitted on a modern Japanese machine with ribber

trated above, follows. The sample was knitted on a chunky machine. In the Harrison manual, the stitch appears in a pattern for bedroom slippers:

```
a H3  1  1  0  1  1  0  1  1  0
            1  1  0  1  1  0  1  1  0

b H4  1  1  0  1  1  0  1  1  0
      1  1  0  1  1  0  1  1  0
```

Set MB to normal. RB left normal, right tuck. Carr at right. H3, knit 2 rows. H4 knit 2 rows. On the standard machines, use H5 and H6. For Duomatic, centre for 2 rows, rack to right for 2 rows.

Waste yarn is recommended to machine knitters as in Mrs Leach's hand-knit patterns. The knitter is advised to use a thicker piece of yarn to throw off the stitches. The decreasings on a collar are quite complicated. The pattern writer does not tell us how they are achieved, but neither would his or her counterpart today. Most, but not all, the garments are dropped shoulder line (see Chapter 8). Like the patterns in *Mrs Leach's Fancy Work-Basket*, there is only one size, but a chart of sizes is provided with all the relevant information presented in a precise form, heralding the more economical system of the 1980s. Apart from an inadequate drawing repre-

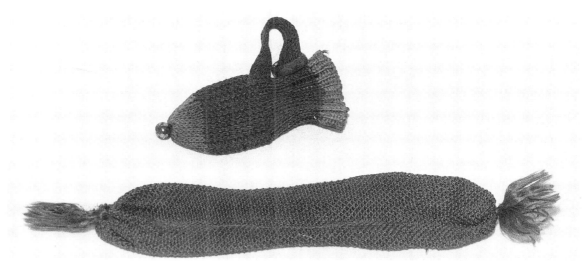

Fig 25

A Victorian machine-knitted pence jug and hand-knitted silk purse

senting a sock, there is no visual aid to accompany the photo or drawing of the finished article.

Patterns for machine-knitted articles were confined, by and large, to the manuals for the machines. These often ran to several volumes to provide supplementary garment and stitch patterns. Machine knitting was regarded as mainly a semi-industrial occupation, although the discovery of a machine-knitted pence jug in the collection of York Castle Museum does indicate that there were some Victorian machine knitters who took pleasure in creating miniature knitted articles. Nevertheless, the number of machine knitters would be very small compared to the great army of home needle crafters.

By the end of the century there were signs that the knitting machine could enhance the status of women and not diminish it. There is an interesting account by J. W. Harrison, of the firm of that name, of the domestic hosiery industry in England and Scotland, and of its extension in Ireland in the *Journal of Agriculture III No. 2*, 1903. It appears that Harrison's marketing success does not go further south than Lancashire although he may, of course, have been limited by the terms of his import licences: 'A large number of the people in the rural centres of Durham, Northumberland, Yorkshire and Lancashire, carry on this industry in their homes with often only a single machine.'

The Irish proved just as quick at learning how to use the knitting machine as their English and Scots counterparts. The writer quotes the example of a 16-year-old girl whose father bought her a machine at the Cork exhibition of 1902. Eventually, the girl proved so successful that she had four machines and provided work for six or seven girls in her area.

It seems, too, that the modern craft fair had its antecedents in 1902:

'There is also another system of pushing sales in vogue which requires a little more time and attention, viz, attending the country fairs or markets in the villages or towns within a certain radius of their homes. They carry a portable stall whereon their goods are displayed along with one or two wicker or cane skits in which their stock is carried.'

As far as patterns for hand and machine knitters were concerned, then, by 1900 there was no sign of a generally accepted abbreviated code nor of a tension swatch, and the diagram seemed a long way away. Instead, the authors of hand- and machine-knitting literature talked to their knitters in a conversational manner and explained in the fullest possible written terms, while visualising was left to the imagination of those who used the patterns.

THREE

The pattern diagram

Dr Gustav Jaeger's claim to fame is that he promoted 'sanitary underwear' and the wearing of natural undyed wool next to the skin. This promotion coincided with the sports boom of the 1880s/ 90s and the movement for healthy living. George Bernard Shaw was a devotee, and for his constitutional jog down London's Regent Street wore a pair of knitted woollen combinations, looking for all the world like 'a forked radish.'

Long combinations were complicated to knit and to shape. Furthermore, they had to fit and be comfortable. There are patterns for both hand- and machine-knitted versions in manuals but these garments must have been difficult for the novice to knit. In *The Girl's Own Paper* (December 1916) there is an advert for ladies' knitted knickers which one could have made to order by the Harrison Knitting Machine Company, presumably by their outworkers. In *The Knitters' Circular and Monthly Record* (December 1895) there are drawings of parts of a pair of combinations with the sections marked alphabetically. The accompanying article explains to industrial machine knitters that they will have to work out each section separately, and in order, and then calculate the number of needles required and subsequent shaping. The whole pre-knitting approach is remarkably modern and sounds familiar to a machine knitter of today. 'Any size or gauge of article should be made by a careful study of the proportions given.'

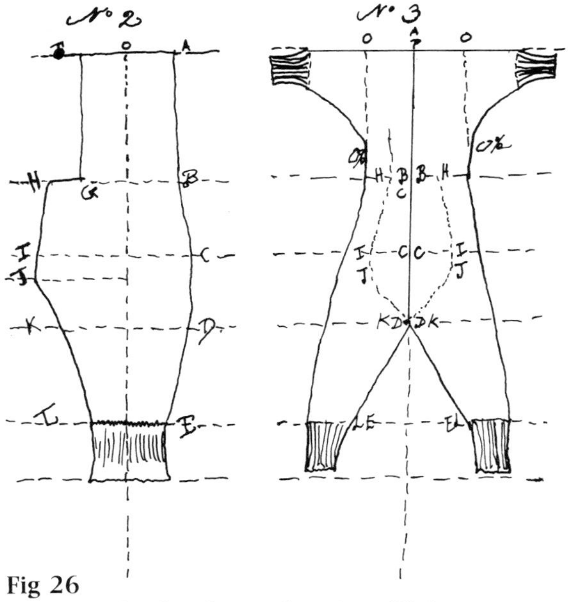

A new type of manual

In actual fact, drawings had appeared earlier but not with popular recipes. The Education Acts of 1870 and after spawned a new type of needlecraft manual – the hardback, comprehensive reference book for teachers and students. At the end of Amy K. Smith's *Needlework for Student Teachers* (1894), the requirements of the needlework code for schools are printed. These include the principles of knitting that are to be taught and practised.

The most difficult task to be given to standard five pupils was 'to knit the heel of a stocking, turn it and cast off'. No knitting instruction was compulsory beyond standard five, but the teaching of needlework was a statutory requirement in standard six. Elizabeth Rosevear's *Needlework, Knitting, Cutting Out* (Macmillan, 1893) accompanies a sizing chart for stockings with a primitive little

Fig 26
Garment sketches for combinations (Knitters Circular and Monthly Record, December 1895)

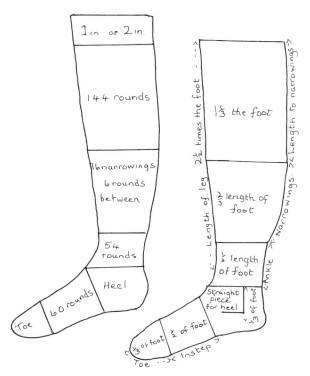

Fig 27
Drawings for a personalized, hand-knitted stocking pattern (TM James, 1901)

sketch of a stocking. Elizabeth Rosevear also had the following advice for teachers: 'Sewing and knitting machines cannot be disregarded, because they are in more general use than a few years ago.' Her book contains some beautiful stitch patterns for older children to try on two needles. This teaching inspired the knitting of lace edgings for mats, pillowcases, tray, and table, cloths. There were no instructions for designing and knitting sweaters or jackets.

The best examples of charts that I can find are in T. M. James's *Complete Course of Needlework, Knitting and Cutting Out* (Longmans, 1901), where one of two stocking drawings is divided into sections and annotated with the number of rounds and narrowings. The other drawing shows the sections given as proportions. Working out breakdowns by proportions and developing them into a method for personalized design has had a considerable following among knitters in the West (see Chapter 9).

The gentleman's waistcoat

What is so striking about these manuals is that there are plenty of diagrams for the dressmaking sections but not one, except for stockings, in the knitting section. We have to wait for the knitting as dressmaking approach popular in the 1920s to 1930s. There was, however, one remarkable garment which truly defeated the shaping ability of

Fig. 28
Flora Klickman's gentleman's waistcoat

hand and machine knitters from the eighteenth century onwards, and that was the gentleman's waistcoat with pointed and/or curved fronts. In the eighteenth century, as I have said, frame-knitted waistcoats were cut and sewn. Here is the advice in the *Ladies' Knitting Book* (first series, 1883), for hand knitters who wanted to knit a gentleman's waistcoat in moss stitch: 'When you have knitted it long enough, work another side in the same manner, and send it to a tailor to make up. This knitting will not run down when cut, as the stitches can be taken up with ease if carefully done.'

In Weldon's *Shilling Guide to Fancywork* (1914–16) too, there is a waistcoat, this time knitted in two colours. The instructions, however, could be from 1883: 'This waistcoat is made in two straight pieces, shaping being left to the tailor, a method much more satisfactory for making up and much easier to work than attempting to shape during the working.'

What defeated the hand and machine knitters of the eighteenth and nineteenth centuries was exactly the same problem that defeats many British knitters today: how to calculate and shape on the bias when the line is critical. The two, curved fronts of the waistcoat provide us with a classic example of simple bias knitting. The hand knitter of 1883 and 1914 had to send her knitted pieces to the tailor to cut and make up because she didn't know how to fashion the correct shape by increasing and decreasing. Moreover, she wanted a lined garment which would firm the fabric and make it look like cloth. This dressmaking tradition has a small but enthusiastic following among machine knitters today.

In *The Textile Industries, Vol. 7* by William Murphy (Gresham, 1911), we read how industrial knitters tackled the waistcoat: 'The finishing of waistcoats is a special line of work requiring the skill of the tailor. The fronts are lined, buttons sewn on, and the backs cut and made as in any tailoring establishment.'

Flora Klickman, editor of *The Girl's Own Paper* and *Woman's Magazine*, also edited *The Modern Knitting Book* (1916) where there is a pattern for a shaped moss stitch, flannel-lined waistcoat with an accompanying diagram, reproduced here. At some time between 1883 and 1916, hand knitters had

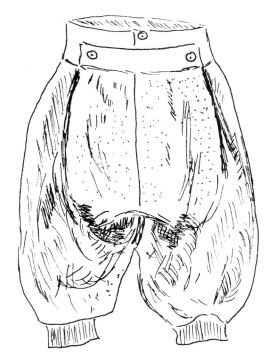

Fig 29
The back view of a pair of ladies' sports knickers. Each pair needed 26ozs DK wool, 5 buttons and sateen for the band (Flora Klickman, 1916)

discovered how to shape the waistcoat front, at least in one kind of yarn and one kind of stitch, *i.e.* moss stitch.

Flora Klickman's pattern format is so strikingly modern that one must ask what happened to British hand knitting? Why didn't it continue in the diagrammatic way? The waistcoat pattern could almost be from a modern Japanese manual: 'Except for the first few rows of both halves of the waistcoat, no detailed directions are given, as the sketch shows the positions and numbers of increases, decreases and main stitches.'

The appearance of abbreviations

Abbreviations for knitting instructions appeared in the first decade of the twentieth century. They do not seem to have been employed consistently for quite a few years, and each author tended to have her own code. Richard Rutt writes that Jane Gaugain invented a set of abbreviations as early as the 1840s, but those used in Weldon's *Practical Needlework* (1906) were the ones which eventually gained general acceptance. The earliest abbreviations I have in my collection are in the pattern for coloured garter stitch in *Mrs Leach's Fancy Work-Basket* (1886). Here the names of the colours are abbreviated to one letter each.

A number of writers used abbreviations, as Flora Klickman does, to give the sequence of the stitch pattern, but wrote the general directions out in full. Flora Klickman provides a key to the abbreviations used in the patterns; O for over, N for narrow, and so on. Unfortunately, there are no other diagram patterns in her book. The waistcoat pattern is a rarity. There is, however, some rather different advice for people wanting to knit garments of their own choice:

> 'The worker will find it a good plan to work to a flat pattern, cut in paper or muslin, of the particular garment required. If you have a pattern before you that has been fitted to the wearer, it is quite a simple matter to shape your work to this, by increasing or decreasing stitches to get the necessary slopes required.'

Notice that there is no appeal to mathematics. Flora Klickman must have been the original 'shape as you knit' expert, but how would her vague advice fare with today's post-knit culture generation? I suspect, however that she wouldn't have known how to pattern-write the breakdowns for a sleeve cap, and she certainly wouldn't have understood how they were accomplished.

Flora Klickman also has advice on the practice, current at the time, of using four needles for large body garments like jerseys and long stockings, and two needles for smaller pieces of knitting. In Weldon's *Shilling Guide to Fancy Work* (1914–16), for example, we read: 'Knitting on two needles is sometimes called a flat web. This kind is most used in edgings though sometimes articles are knit in this way and then sewed together, as, for instance, breadths of petticoats.'

Larger-scale flat knitting was not far away, however, and in another 10–15 years would supplant knitting in the round as the way to knit fashion garments. In the meantime, neither Flora Klickman nor Weldon's *Shilling Guide* mentions

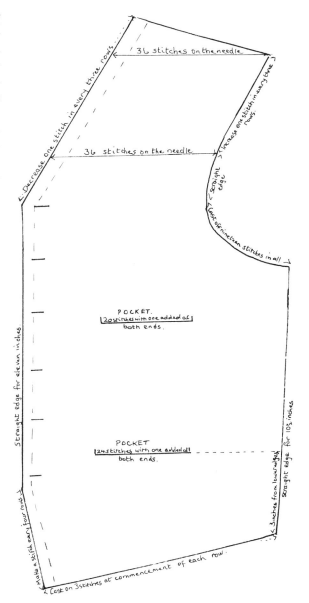

Fig 30
Flora Klickman's 'working diagram' for a gentleman's waistcoat (1916)

stitch or row gauge. That again is the subject for the 1920s and '30s, and even then most writers were only interested in number of stitches per inch, as indeed are many hand knitters of today.

The First World War and after

The First World War altered everything. Its appalling carnage resulted in a lost generation of men. Women who had filled their menfolk's jobs during the war found that they continued to keep them after the conflict was over. They became heads of the first one-parent families and, like their successors 70 years later, didn't appear to knit much. Women were given the vote at last, and needlecrafts were neglected as leisure-time pursuits. For many, needlecrafts were a symbol of domestic drudgery and a former lowly status. Others, it seems, were knitting sweaters in response to the jumper craze of the 1920s. A decade later, in the preface to *Modern Needlecraft* (Blackie, 1932), David Mintner wrote: 'Needlecraft is coming back into its own. In every part of the country there is a revival of interest in decorative stitchery – embroidery, knitting, crocheting – as well as in the more practical forms of sewing.'

His book was for 'the creative woman', and had a very different design and pattern emphasis from previous manuals.

In the collection of the Gallery of English Costume, Platt Hall, Manchester, there are a surprising number of machine-knitted jerseys and suits *c*.1920, which indicate very clearly that the first knitwear that could be called 'fashion' was machine knitted. I have a 1920s manual for the

Fig 31
A machine-knitted coat of the early 1920s worked in embossed striped double jacquard

Fig 32
*Machine-knit fashion for the home knitter –
a ladies' 'costume', c.1925 (Foster)*

domestic machine which includes patterns for elegant suits. The yarns recommended are industrial 2/16s wool, *i.e.* 2 ply, and not hand-knit balled yarns, which indicates that a coned yarn industry would be required for machine knitting in due course. Thereafter we hear little of machine knitting as a domestic craft in the next 30 years. The circular sock machine continued to be popular, and the domestic, hand-powered, V-bed was indispensable in small knitwear concerns. The following comment appeared in an advertisement in an issue of the *Needlecraft Practical Journal*, *c.*1922:

> 'The new Harrison flat knitter is the best machine possible for knitting costumes, dresses, jumpers, coats, boys' suits, socks, stockings etc . . . The knitting industry is an excellent branch for young women starting in business as there has been an increasing demand for knitted goods in recent years, and this demand is likely to continue as knitted goods are so comfortable in all weathers.'

What women needed most of all was a different style of dressing to suit their new energetic role in society. York Castle Museum has in its collection a machine-knitted trouser suit, *c.*1920, which must have matched the mood of the moment. The Leicester Museum has machine-knitted articles from this period while the Victoria and Albert Museum, London, has an elegant cut and sewn, machine-knitted coat, *c.*1925. It is not always possible to determine whether machine-knitted articles in museum collections were knitted in a domestic or industrial environment, though cut and sew was a more industrial technique.

Gabrielle 'Coco' Chanel

One report from the Nottingham/Leicester area tells us that in the early 1920s a French designer bought some fine cashmere and silk and wool men's undershirts from an English firm which was making them on handframes. The designer remodelled the garments and trimmed them with crêpe de chine to become women's jerseys. Modern industrial sources in Leicester confirm that this designer was Chanel. Shortly afterwards, beautiful, elegant, easy-to-wear suits by Chanel appeared in

the fashion glossies. This was the day when one dressed to suit the occasion. For evenings, Chanel used knitted jersey woven with gold or silver, an innovation which caused nearly as much furore as did the 'New Look' in 1947. In the 1920s, one was not supposed to acknowledge a need for comfort as well as elegance in outerwear. Chanel and her arch-rival in the 1930s, Schiaparelli, changed all that. It was, therefore, natural that women knitting at home would want to interpret this new, comfortable outer fashion in their own medium. Already they were engaged in a different kind of knitting.

Fair Isle and folk knitting

The Fair Isle boom of the 1920s made folk knitting fashionable, and highlighted the need for written communication of the traditional oral patterns. Traditional knitting, *i.e.* Fair Isle, gansey and later Aran, became a genre in its own right, even though the tradition was in most cases less than a hundred years old. For the first time magazines, pattern leaflets and, later, books, featured 'traditional' patterns. Knitting in the round with four needles continued to be the method recommended for the Fair Isle styles in homecraft magazines for at least several years before flat knitting with two needles finally took over. The appeal of Fair Isle and Aran was, and is, to romanticism, and for a time, until historians challenged some of the more questionable myths, the financial rewards for the perpetrators were considerable. A generation weary of war and drained by the Depression was easily swept up on a wave of nostalgia for the idyllic handicrafts of the past. No one remembered the harsh realities of life in those times.

The 1920s represent an interim period. Abbreviations and stitch and row tensions appeared in some patterns but not in others. There was hardly a diagram in sight.

Marjory Tillotson

If hand knitters wanted to blame machine knitters for some of the pattern confusion they have inherited they would be quite justified in doing so. The first knitted fashions in the 1920s were machine knitted and many were cut and sewn. When the new vogue was interpreted for the women's magazines as hand knitting to shape, only a few freelance designer-writers realized that the differences in the construction of woven and knitted fabrics were crucial and that there was a clear relationship to consider between the stitch and the row in the interpretation of the pattern. One of the most influential knitting designers and authorities was Marjory Tillotson. She worked for Baldwins long before their merger with Patons in 1920, and was responsible for many issues of *Woolcraft*. However, for all its tremendous influence throughout the years there was not one garment diagram in any issue of *Woolcraft*. Neither were there any patterns for ladies' sweaters and jackets until the issues of 1929–30 (see Chapter 8). If Marjory Tillotson had not also been a freelance writer, and therefore independent of any yarn company, she would have received little mention in this book.

I have in my collection a copy of *Modern Needlecraft* (1932), to which Marjory Tillotson contributed the knitting section, and her *The Complete Knitting Book* (1934). The latter was immensely popular and went into many editions. Indeed, it was still in print in 1967, an indication of its great influence and usefulness. I am in no doubt that the Japanese found it an invaluable reference book. In the preface to *Modern Needlecraft* the editor, David Mintner writes that in the revival of needlecrafts, a woman would want to express her own personality:

> 'It is not enough to choose from amongst the ready-made; she wishes to be able to translate her own ideas into actuality . . . In the knitting and crochet sections a new principle is introduced whereby garments can be knitted to exact measurements from simple diagrams, and any pattern or design can be set down in chart form to be worked without need of the usual detailed instructions.'

All that sounds remarkably modern and indeed Marjory Tillotson's work has played a significant role in promoting the use of both diagrams and symbols (see Chapter 5). For knitwear shapes, she recommends that the garment outline be drawn on graph paper, one square to equal one inch. For a baby's jacket, she advises that we knit a tension swatch over 30 stitches to achieve six and a half stitches per inch. She does not mention rows, but no doubt this is understood by the knitter who would have to interpret the vertical measurement in rows. It seems, then, that only a part of the problem had been solved.

Marjory Tillotson eventually realized the obstacles she faced, and one wonders what lay behind the remarks in the introduction to her publication *The Complete Knitting Book*, first published two years after her contribution to *Modern Needlecraft*:

> 'Unfortunately, far too many knitters rely upon stereotyped directions and designs and copy slavishly these printed patterns. As there is so much difference between the work of one knitter and another, two garments knitted to the same instructions seldom come out to the

Fig 33
'The ideal jumper for the middle-aged woman' –
a typical garment of the mid-1930s

same size. These stereotyped instructions, given in knitting books, do not always work out to the required measurements, and what is more, LEAVE NO SCOPE FOR ORIGINALITY.'

The emphasis is hers. It was as if Marjory Tillotson was both apologising for and renouncing all the earlier work she had done in *Woolcraft* for over 20 years. If anyone had been responsible for establishing the written no-diagram pattern as a way of life, it was her. This therefore shows a complete reversal of approach.

In her book Marjory Tillotson has remembered the rows. Both stitch and row tensions are given and she tells us how to measure the trial piece/ swatch. She understands how to shape on the bias, how to use short rows and how to calculate, but does not know the Magic Formula (see Chapter 4). 'It will be found that the numbers do not always divide exactly and the nearest approximate number must be reckoned.' The pattern format is revolutionary and has much in common with that of the modern Japanese. The writing, however, is reserved for advice on how to work out your own requirements. There are no breakdowns marked on the diagram.

Mary Thomas and after

Marjory Tillotson was followed by the more famous Mary Thomas. Although the section on garment design is the least convincing part of her otherwise

excellent *Knitting Book* (1938), Mary Thomas does give a warning about treating knitted fabric as if it were woven. The growing tendency, she says, is to knit from paper patterns, and these seldom have the simplicity of outline necessary for knitted fabric. Even so, to modern eyes her toile is merely a dressmaker's toile with different armhole lengths for back and front. When many of today's young knitwear designers say they know how to draft, they mean for dressmaking, and one is given the impression that they regard the approach as exactly the same for fully-fashioned knit. This misunderstanding is responsible for a great deal of confusion in current knitwear design, and we can trace it back to the teaching of the 1930s.

Mary Thomas's advice on garment design is too generalized and vague. If she does not give precise help on how to deal with breakdowns, then Catherine Franks, in *The Pictorial Guide to Home Knitting* (1939), most certainly does. In fact her drawings of the pattern pieces in this book are stepped to show the row breakdowns. The next time we see row steps, they are on graph paper, where one tiny square represents a stitch horizontally and a row vertically. Apart from Mary Thomas in her *Book of Knitting Patterns* (1943), no one in the early 1940s considered that the stitch and row ratio mostly produced a rectangle and not a square, and that the square graph-paper representation was therefore a distorted image.

The stepped diagram was at least a move in the right direction, because it showed that the designer appreciated that the structured unit of knit was the stitch and that connected horizontal stitches

Fig 34
The Passap D machine (1939)

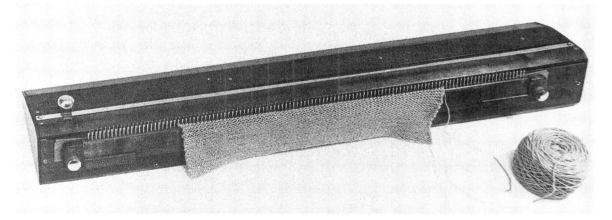

formed serried ranks called rows, which lay above and below in vertical formation. Once a line was drawn on the graph paper, the designer could begin to step either on it or as near to it as possible, and organize the steps so that the increases or decreases fell on knit rows if necessary. The next stage of development can be seen in *Knit and Crochet your own Fashions of the Forties* by Alice Carroll (Dover). Here there is a very modern-looking, graphed-out garment block, featuring a pattern of purl and plain. The block could well be used for modern intarsia and would not be out of place in a pattern collection today.

At the end of the 1930s and beginning of the 1940s, the multi-sized pattern appeared, including two or more sizes and their breakdowns. The knitter was expected not to get confused by having to sort out which numbers were for her size. Being able to cater for more than one size in a pattern was of greater concern to the spinners than teaching

Fig 35
A 1940s jumper. Note the combination of sideways and conventionally knitted stripes

knitters to fend for themselves. The impression was firmly given that it was the knitter's duty to follow the pattern. The spinners' legitimate concern was selling yarn, not personalized design. Certainly, there were some attractive sweater patterns in the 1940s. The fitted sleeve design was the most popular, and the stitch patterns were really quite beautiful.

After the Second World War, the movement towards personalized design came to a halt in British pattern literature produced by freelance authors. In *Knitting for All Illustrated* by Margaret Murray and Jane Koster (Odhams, 1941) there is some advice for using a block pattern on personalized design, but that advice and its accompanying diagram disappeared from publications by these two authors after 1945. It was as if a censor had been at work and drawn a curtain quite deliberately across personal creativity in this area. Although freelance designers continued to give advice on personalized design using the block and stepped, square-gridded graph paper, hardly any new ideas have been forthcoming until very recently. Maggie Whiting has a refreshing experimental approach in *The Progressive Knitter* (Batsford, 1988) while Montse Stanley, a Catalan from Spain, shows hand knitters the necessity of proportional graphing in *Knitting Your Own Designs for a Perfect Fit* (David and Charles, 1982).

New developments in the USA

Some of the most interesting and innovative developments in hand and machine knitting in the last 25 years have come from North Americans living either in their native land or in Britain. In hand knitting there are at least four outstanding personalities: Barbara Walker for her work with charting methods and stitch patterns, many of the latter her own creations; British-born Elizabeth Zimmerman for her highly individual approach to garment design for ordinary knitters, and Mary Walker Phillips for raising hand knitting to the level of an art form; but perhaps the most famous British-American knitter is Kaffe Fassett, whose missionary zeal and exquisite sense of colour and pattern have ensured an honoured place for hand knitting in many a fashion collection.

Fig 36
'Sheep in Wolf's Clothing', machine-knitted on the chunky machine by Judith Duffey

Compared to the situation in Britain, machine knitting in North America is still a minority interest. That it has come so far is due in no small way to the teaching-design work of the German-Canadian, Regine Faust. The American Susanna Lewis must be one of the most creative and knowledgeable machine knitters anywhere in the world, while the British-American Judith Duffey is making us aware of machine knitting as an art form with her strange, haunting, free-standing sculptures.

North America has been the recipient of many knitting traditions which have come together in its melting-pot culture. This situation has resulted in an urge to explore new areas and a willingness to accept innovation.

British Designer publications

The Knitwear Revolution which began in the late 1970s spawned an entirely new kind of lavishly illustrated pattern book which provided constant inspiration for use of colour and pattern mainly on

Fig 37
'Life-cycle of the monarch butterfly'. A cape wall-hanging worked in machine knitting, crochet and applique by Susanna Lewis

the dropped shoulder line shape. Although it was all very exciting and exhilarating, the movement could not halt the decline of popular knitting. Indeed, by fixing a gulf between designer and artisan knitter, the movement made the decline inevitable. On the credit side, the designers responsible were breaking old moulds and exploring areas of colour and surface pattern in a new and exciting way. With few exceptions, they were not interested in technique, nor in the presentation of knitwear as a design discipline where structural components were as crucial as surface and colour. Their mission was to banish the 'granny image' in knitting. Perhaps this was necessary, and certainly the liberation has had a beneficial effect. Unfortunately, in their enthusiasm many got rid of some of granny's technical skills as well.

Because the designer books emphasize colour and surface pattern, intarsia and Fair Isle charts are common, but the attitude towards the knitter is patronising, while personalized design information, except in one or two notable exceptions, is conspicuous by its absence.

The diagram and contemporary machine knitting

The patterns which were published by the machine manufacturers in the 1950s and early 1960s, followed the hand-knit pattern format very closely. After all, the same yarn was used by both hand and machine knitters (and resulted in some rather stiff-looking garments in the magazines for machine knitters). The first issue of Knitmaster's *Modern Knitting* appeared in December 1955. In those days, two- and three-ply balled yarns were still plentiful and so one could produce beautiful effects, especially with the ribber and double-bed machines. Multi-size patterns were common; the tension gauge was given in stitches and rows per inch and there were no diagrams. The exception to the rule was provided by Passap of Switzerland. I have several copies of the Passap pattern book which appeared for the M201 machine in the mid-1950s. The quality of the patterns is very high indeed. The gauge in stitches and rows is for two inches. Yarns are not branded, and only one size, with measurements, is given. The most revolutionary part of the pattern is the clear garment diagram with measurements in inches and centimetres. Each part of the block is marked with a letter and these sections are referenced in the written recipe, which makes following each process a visual, as well as a knitting, matter. Knitters could see exactly where they had got to in their knitting. This approach immediately set them apart from their hand-knitting contemporaries.

The Passap Duomatic machine was first launched in 1961, and two years later the Model Books began to come out twice yearly from Switzerland. It wasn't very long before the Model Books became famous for the superb quality of their garment designs and the visual aid offered by the garment patterns, this time not only with measurements but with breakdowns given in the house code of the Passap company. This code is still in use, and is, in fact, very close to the Japanese method of writing breakdowns which came before it. At the back of the early Model Books, ready-reckoner charts were given to convert the one-size pattern into any stitch and row multiples of your choosing. *The Passap ABC* (1975), which gives help on garment design, also demonstrates the use of the Passap system in pattern making.

British knitters, on the whole, never took to the charts. One who did, and who explained them with her legendary clarity, was Mary Weaver in her book *The Passap Duomatic* (1974). Mary Weaver is the visionary architect of modern machine knitting. She was also one of the first writers to establish a strong private publishing tradition in machine knitting. At the beginning of the 1970s, when she went to Courtaulds, the industrial yarn producers, and asked for coned yarn, her request was met with incredulity. Ever since Patons had begun to advertise their yarns for hand and machine knitters at the beginning of the twentieth century, the major spinners had assumed that machine knitters used the same yarns as hand knitters. Mary Weaver was sent to the yarn merchants F. W. Bramwell, who are now the largest supplier of branded coned yarn to the domestic machine-knitting industry in the English-speaking world. The yarns that machine knitting prefer are waxed and more loosely twisted than those for hand knitting.

At the beginning of her book *The Passap Duomatic*, Mary Weaver gives a masterly survey of the knitwear scene in the early 1970s as she saw it, persuading and cajoling those frightened of the machines to approach the task of learning with confidence. She introduces knitters to the pattern format she is to use in subsequent publications and which I have adapted and followed in my own writing. Industrial counts of yarn are introduced to knitters. Her patterns are multi-size but plenty of space is taken to spread the numbers across the page. Each pattern has a diagram annotated with breakdowns as well as with measurements. I have adapted this dual approach to recipes for my own purpose.

We have been working through an interim period serving two kinds of knitters, those who feel happy with the written word, and those who prefer the economy and the visual aid provided by the pattern diagram. Now is the time for a radical new approach.

The Japanese influence

In the mid-1960s, the Japanese push-button machines arrived in the West. At the end of 1967, the same year in which the Japanese Industrial Standards committee ratified its code for knitting publications in Japan, garment diagrams annotated with measurements suddenly appeared in Knitmaster's *Modern Knitting* and then in Jones & Brother's *Stitch in Time*. The punchcard machines appeared in 1971 and took over the market. 1972 was a memorable year. The first charting device

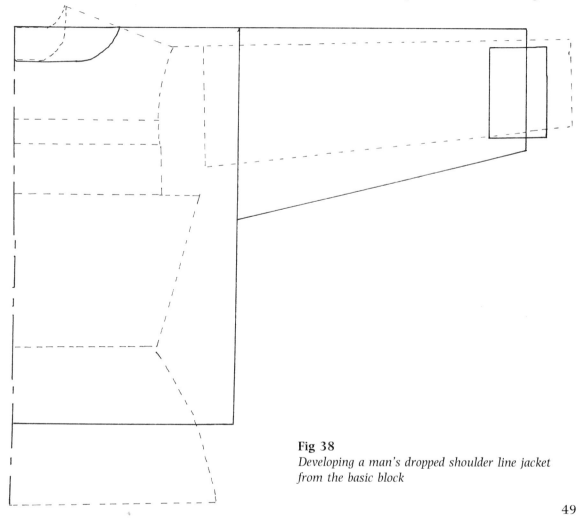

Fig 38
Developing a man's dropped shoulder line jacket from the basic block

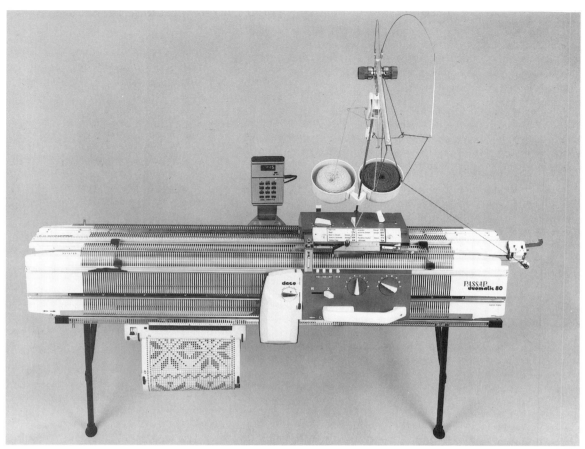

Fig 39
*The Passap Duomatic 80 (1983) with deco and
form computer*

Fig 40
*Knitmaster 360 punchcard machine (1980)
showing built-in Knitradar charting device*

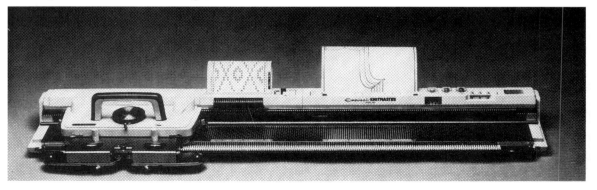

(known also as the charter), the Knitmaster Knitradar, arrived in Britain from Japan, followed by the Brother Knitleader, the Toyota KnitTracer, and the Passap Superba Pattern Driver. The Passap authorities were never happy with the Pattern Driver and moved on to promote the Form Computer, a type of calculator programmed by the manufacturer in a code the knitter is not meant to understand. Unlike the charting device, the Form Computer offers limited scope for personalized design but is at its best dealing with basic shapes or with those offered by the manufacturer, whose numbers one enters without comprehension. The knitter can, of course, choose from a variety of stitch patterns.

There is no doubt that various computerized aids to garment pattern making are on the way and these may well have a growing acceptance in the mass market.

Fig 41
A Japanese knitting student using full-scale Knitleader on a Brother punchcard machine

Magazines for machine knitters

Today, virtually all pattern publications carry diagrams alongside the written recipes, but the situation is a confused one. Multi-sized patterns are common, but many knitters use the diagrams as the basis for their own designs, which they draw for the charting device. They can then knit in a stitch and row gauge of their choosing. There are quite a few British magazine publications for machine knitters. Each magazine has its own house language, and there seems to be no move at all towards a common system. At the time of writing, Knitmaster's *Modern Machine Knitting* is the only magazine which uses a diagrammatic code based on the Japanese system, but there is an ongoing debate on diagrams in *Machine Knitting News*, which has the largest circulation of any monthly for machine knitters. Moreover, the latest *Machine Knitting News European Collection*, a separate publication, uses for the first time the diagrammatic format popularized by Passap, because the magazine is to be translated into several languages for

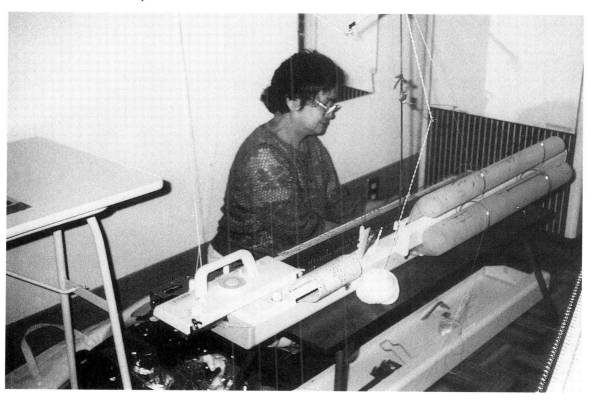

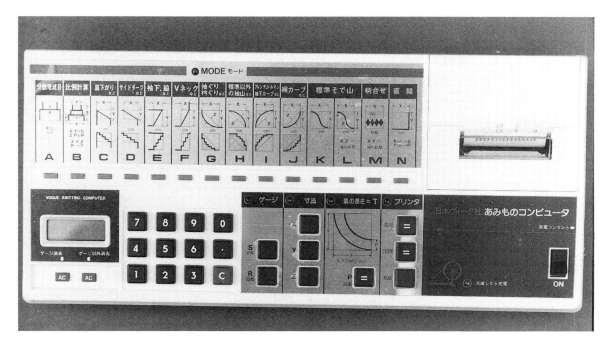

Fig 42
Nihon Vogue knitting computer

the international market. The differences between the Passap and Japanese formats are slight, but the overwhelming majority of machine knitters use the latter. Certainly, with the City and Guilds examination course and the Japanese system being taught in colleges throughout Britain, the case for diagrams is being put more strongly than ever. If hand knitters choose to dissociate themselves from the movement, then one wonders what the future will hold for them.

FOUR

The Japanese pattern format

In the *Knitting Machine Instruction Manual* by Hanae Okamoto, published in English by the Josei no Tomo Co Ltd, Tokyo, in 1957, there is no evidence that the designers knew the line sum method we call the 'Magic Formula', and which the City and Guilds scheme for machine knitting calls the 'Diophantine Equation'. The old method of calculating breakdowns and leaving any leftovers to distribute as you please is used, but the patterns are shown in the most economical way and the printed text is left for the technical information. Only one size is given per pattern, and the breakdowns are written Japanese-style on the sketch diagram of the garment pieces. Therefore 6–1–26 means on the sixth row decrease or increase one stitch twenty-six times. On a symmetrical piece like a sleeve the instructions apply to each side.

The Americans and the Magic Formula

I first read about the Magic Formula in *Knitting Pattern Drafting by Charts for Knitting Machine and Handknitting* (published in English by the Okamoto Pub. Co Ltd, Yokohama, 1976) where the Magic Formula is called 'the sum'. However, in *Chart-Rite* by the American authors Bonnie Ralston and Norma Sweet, published by the authors in 1974, various applications of 'the formula' (no Magic) are used for all the breakdown calculations. The authors speak of the 'Japanese formulas' as if the Americans were well-accustomed to using them. Susanna Lewis, the American machine knitting authority, described in *Fashion and Craft* (March 1988), how the Magic Formula got its name. It was first used in 1975 by the American writer and editor Alles Hutchinson in her book *Charting by the*

Magic Formula. In the revized edition, 1983, the author explains further:

> 'Through studying books describing how to chart, all of which had been printed in Japan, one little piece of information kept cropping up. A mathematical calculation was being used over and over again which was unfamiliar to me and which was not referred to in the books. Whatever it was it certainly worked. Finally I gave it a name: The Magic Formula.'

Alles Hutchinson traces the formula back to Diophantos, a Greek mathematician *c.*500 AD, who presented remainders as integers or whole numbers.

The British and the Magic Formula

Open discussion of the Magic Formula in *Fashion and Craft* and *Slip Knot* has highlighted two important questions for hand and machine knitters in Britain:

1. When did the Japanese, who have no knitting culture to speak of, discover this quite remarkable and foolproof method? Certainly the Japanese Industrial Standards Committee endorsed its use in 1967.

2. Why have British hand knitters only just heard of it when British, American and South African machine-knit authors have been explaining the use of the formula for nearly 15 years? There is a simple answer to the second question. Hand knitters have considered that what happens in machine knitting is of no concern to them, whereas in actual fact the two knitting crafts

have a common approach to pattern design.

Because the formula sum really does open a door on a whole new world of design and practice, the Americans and then the British, following Alles Hutchinson's example, began to call it 'magic', a more accurate description is 'a line sum'.

The Magic Formula is the basis for breakdowns in Japanese computer programs for garment patterns. An example of the sum is given in the manual for the Nihon Vogue Knit Computer. The Magic Formula is also the basis on which the charting device works. In any attempt to interpret a diagonal line accurately in pattern breakdowns, the Magic Formula is the means by which it is done.

Definition

The Magic Formula/line sum/Diophantine equation is a long-division sum in which the remainders are shown as integers or whole numbers and not as fractions of the divisor. The sum is set down in an established way, with arrows to show the connections between the various parts. In the old way of calculating stitch increases on the rows of the underarm seam, any leftovers would be tacked on at the end. The sequences would be arranged quite arbitrarily without any reference to the line that was prescribed. When we are in personal charge of our pattern making and don't rely on computers or on a charting device, we find there are three main expressions of the formula. Some authorities would say there are two, but I find that this does not give sufficient coverage to all aspects.

1. For the regular decrease or increase of stitches in rows along a diagonal, as on underarm seams, V-necks, darts, raglans and bias knitting of any kind, *i.e.* knitting diagonally from corner to corner. In this expression there is always a hidden right-angled triangle on one side of the diagonal. In each case, the diagonal is the hypotenuse of the triangle. Where a design is complicated and two or more diagonals can be seen along a line, then the triangles need to be traced in and the sum worked out for each stage.

2a. For the even distribution of extra stitches which have to be decreased or increased for

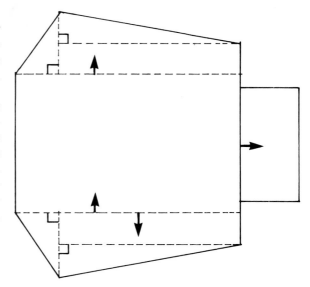

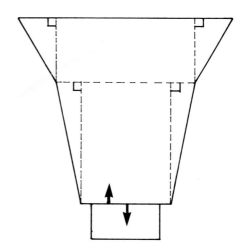

Fig 43
The hidden right-angled triangles on two different sleeve designs

features like cuffs, peplums, waistbands and yoked sweaters.

2b. For even distribution of stitches/rows in buttonhole bands and for distributing shaping groups of stitches along the length of a sideways-knitted skirt.

3. For the creation of flares and mitres using the short row technique, and in skirts, polygon

knitting and sideways knitted circular yokes, as well as for breakdowns for colour changes in holding-position, geometric, intarsia. This particular technique of shaping usually involves breakdowns every other row.

The Japanese diagrammatic code

Before looking at any examples closely it is necessary to understand the code the Japanese use on their diagrams. For that reason a page from a Nihon Vogue pattern book has been reproduced here. These symbols relate to the diagrams and are not the universal ones for stitch patterns. Because machine knitters have the option of drawing the block for the charting device, usually only half the block is shown. A vertical, broken line composed of long and short bars denotes a fold. The unbracketed figures are measurements in centimetres. When there is an arrow at the end only of the line across the neck edge, then the measurement and stitches refer to the complete length and not just to the half you see on the block. The larger arrows within the diagram point to the direction of knitting. D is tension for the tension dial on the machine. In their patterns the Japanese rarely give the three-figure breakdown sum for the reduction of stitches for the welt or a cuff. The knitter is expected to work it out. B/O means bind off, *i.e.* cast off. Where waste yarn is used for casting on, hand knitters are expected to knit from a crocheted chain in contrast yarn.

Paired breakdown sequences

It is important to realize that when the Japanese print rows of treble breakdowns at one side of the sleeve neckline, the figures refer to each other. They usually begin with the number to increase or decrease immediately. On the armhole cutout, the first row repeated will be a purl row for hand knitters. You are expected to know by the shape of the block whether you increase or decrease or cast on or off as the case may be. The pattern format also assumes knowledge of basic procedures, so on a neckline you are supposed to know what to do with the stitches you are holding. In machine knitting, don't cast off the centre stitches, hold them on

waste yarn. In hand knitting I use the welt size needles for waste yarn knitting and return to the practice Mrs Leach recommended in 1886, except that I wouldn't use 'coarse wool of any kind', (see p. 36).

The conventional way to do short row sequences is on every other row, beginning with the first row and thereafter every alternate row. The numbers 2–6–10, therefore, mean hold 6 stitches every alternate row 10 times (opposite the carriage for machine knitters).

The Japanese frequently fill up spaces on patterns by showing on a drawing or photograph how one does a particular process. (No doubt initially this kind of visual material would be expensive to produce, but once the pattern publisher has a full set of illustrations these can be used again and again.) Please refer to the list of technical books recommended for hand and machine knitters at the end of this book if you are unsure which technique to employ. With reference to my own garment designs (Chapter 6 onwards), to keep the pattern presentation simple and to highlight the format, I give only minimal technical information. The Japanese would perhaps be a little more generous, but not much.

Examples from Nihon Vogue publications

By kind permission of Nihon Vogue, I have reproduced two examples from their former machine knitting magazine (English and Japanese instructions) for Spring 1987, and two for hand knitters from *Mohair Knitting* by Rieko Togawa (English only). Once you have understood the principle of the Magic Formula, you will find the patterns most interesting to study and perhaps you will discover eventually that you would prefer not to cope with old, inefficient, ways of pattern making. I have chosen the Japanese patterns to illustrate two expressions of the Magic Formula (see Chapter 10 for a third), but first it is worth drawing attention to the similarities between the format for hand and machine knit patterns. It is quite possible to read and understand both hand and machine knitting patterns even though you are involved only with one craft.

READING THE SHAPING FIGURES

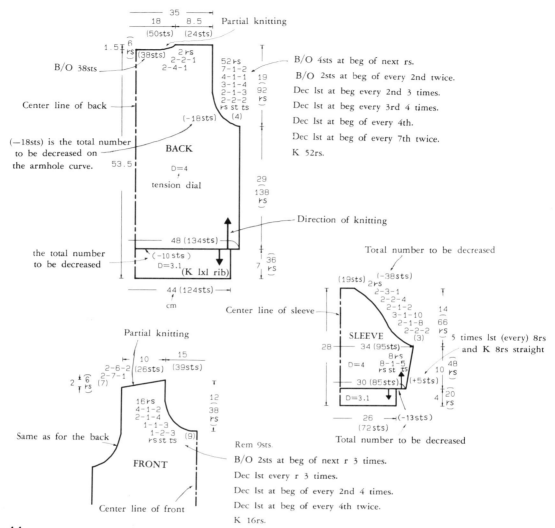

Fig 44
Page from a Nihon Vogue machine-knit pattern book

Expression 1

a. Underarm seam – short sleeve (machine knit). The gauge is not given on this sample page. I work it out as 28sts and 48rs per 10cm (4in). Use a calculator and take the decimal fraction to the nearest whole number. Usually either an odd row is removed or the next higher even number is chosen. The pattern shows that we have to increase 10sts, 5 each side, in 48rs. Now if we divide 48 by 5, the last increase will occur immediately prior to the cast off for the underarm. That makes nonsense, but by adding 1 to the divisor, making it 6, it is possible to ensure that the breakdowns interpret the pattern shape exactly as drawn. The same principle is followed when working out flare breakdowns in skirts. Spaces between buttonholes are more difficult to calculate, because the stitches for the holes themselves must be taken into the calculation.

[32] ★ *Shown on page 66*

Materials: Sport Yarn 330g charcoal gray and 220g off-white. 5 buttons 2.8cm in diameter.

Needles: Knitting needles jumbo 8mm, Nos. 10½ and 9. Crochet hook No. 7.

Sizes: Bust ...106cm. Width across back measurement ...40cm. Length ...56.5cm. Outside sleeve ...53cm.

Gauge: 10 sts and 14.5 rows = 10cm square over stockingette st with charcoal gray and off-white together.

Directions:
● Foundation sts = Make ch sts with another yarn using crochet hook and transfer sts from wrong side of ch to jumbo 8m needles.
● Decreasing over 2 sts = Bind off sts at both sides on 1 row and cut yarn off.
● Decreasing 1 st = Decrease st passing the second st from edge over the first st.
● Increasing st = Cast on new loop next to

the edging st and twist the loop on the following row.
● Joining shoulder seams = Join shoulder seams inside out and fasten off with 1 strand of charcoal gray.
● Shaping cap = Fasten off.
● Lower and wrist band = Bind off.
● Sewing side and sleeve seams = Overcast sts in the center of the edging st.
● Setting sleeve in body = Use half back st with 1 strand of charcoal gray.
● Shoulder pad = See page 81.

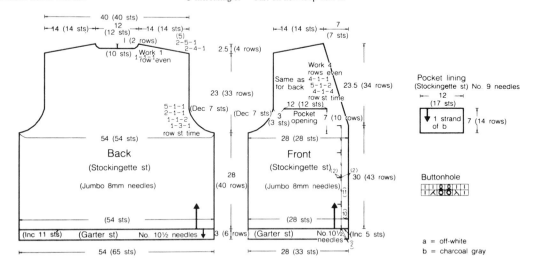

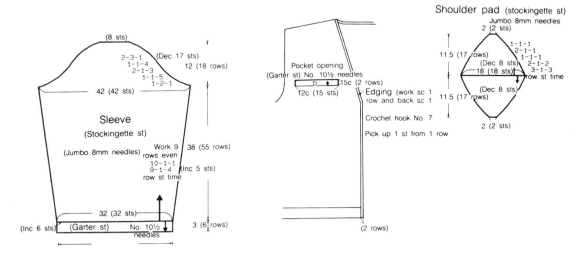

Fig 45
Page from a Nihon Vogue hand-knit pattern book

$$6\,\overline{\smash{\big)}\,48}$$
$$\underline{48}$$
$$00$$
(quotient 8)

Although the divisor is 6, the number of times we increase at each end is 5: hence, the 8–1–5, 8rs written on the diagram. In pattern longhand, we would read, 'Increase 1 stitch at each end of the 8th row 5 times, knit 8 rows'.

b. Underarm seam – long sleeve (hand knit)
This time the tension is worked to a chunky gauge of 10sts and 14.5rs per 10cm (4in). Notice how for a gauge as heavy as this it is necessary to maintain the fraction of 0.5 on the rows for 10cm (4in). Failing to do so means you could end up with a garment that didn't fit. Fractions should not be taken to the next whole number or knocked off in a gauge where the stitch is as large as this. Since your calculator does the sum for you, the fraction should not worry you. Once you have done the measurement translation sum, you can take the stitches and rows to the nearest whole number. So, for the same reasons as described above, you must divide 55rs by 6, not 5. This time the format of the Magic Formula sum will need to be shown in stages:

Stage 1

$$6\,\overline{\smash{\big)}\,55}$$
$$\underline{54}$$
$$1 \text{ rem}$$
(quotient 9)

Stage 2 Put the remainder under the divisor and subtract it because you need to express the remainder as a whole number.

$$6\,\overline{\smash{\big)}\,55}$$
$$\underline{-1 \quad 54}$$
$$5 \quad 1 \text{ rem}$$
(quotient 9)

Stage 3 Now add 1 to the quotient 9 because you have a remainder of 1 which belongs to the next whole quotient of 10 (9 + 1). The arrows show the connection.

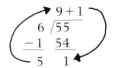

Remember that you have added 1 to the divisor so the 5 will become 4. Now can you understand how the breakdowns are achieved: 9–1–4, 10–1–1, 9 rows? If not, write out groups of 9s in strokes: 111111111 6 times, making 54 in all. Since the dividend is 55, you will have to add the odd 1 to a group of 9 making five nines and one ten. One of the 9s or the 10 refers to straight rows to the armholes. You can arrange the variables to suit your purpose.

c. Front V-neck on hand-knit jacket. Fig 45.
The gauge is the same as **b**. Here we have to reduce 7sts in 34rs, and have the problem of evening-out the breakdowns to give as straight a diagonal as possible within sensible working practice. The divisor is 8 not 7, for the same reason given previously.

$$8\,\overline{\smash{\big)}\,34}$$
$$\underline{-2 \quad 32}$$
$$6 \quad 2$$
(quotient 4 + 1)

As explained in Chapter 4, take one of the fours making the number 5 not 6 to tack on to the top of the V. Here the designer made a decision and there is indeed a choice of arrangement depending on how sharply you want the V to incline: 4–1–4, 5–1–2, 4–1–1, 4rs.

Expression 2

Decrease 10sts evenly from the back for the welt (machine knit pattern, p. 56). We need to make 10sts disappear at regular intervals across 124 needles, or 123 if the base loops are picked up, and have to find out which needles will take 2sts. There can be a choice of variables. To cope with the stitches at the seam edges, I prefer to divide the last group equally and place the first and last decreases the correct distance apart but divided by the seam. In hand knitting the question is, where do we knit or purl 2 together.

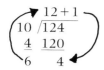

$$\begin{array}{r} 12+1 \\ 10\,\overline{)124} \\ \underline{4}\quad 120 \\ 6\qquad 4 \end{array}$$

Place the extra stitch on the following needles in the sequence: 12th needle – 2sts – 6 times; 13th needle – 2sts – 4 times.

This arrangement won't work for machine knitting, however, because we would have to place the last stitch to be decreased at the extreme edge. The best way is to divide the first group of 12 into 6 at the beginning and 6 at the end. The sequence is as follows: 6th needle, 12th needle × 5, 13th needle × 4, 6 needles, which in Japanese shorthand would read: 6–2–1, 12–2–5, 13–2–4, 6 needles. The distribution can be evened out if desired. Now work out the sum for 123ns.

NB. If you hand knit from the welt upwards, you will obviously be increasing rather than decreasing. The sum, then, would be 114 divided by 10, resulting in the breakdowns of 11–2–6, 12–2–4.

Program for a household calculator

Use the following procedure for the conversion of horizontal and perpendicular measurements in cms on your garment sketch to stitches and rows.

1. Enter the multiplier, *e.g.* stitches per 1 cm.
2. Enter x for times. (Some calculators require x to be pressed twice.)
3. Enter the measurements to be translated to stitches.
4. Press the = sign for the answer.
5. Repeat from **3** until all stitch conversions are complete.
6. Enter the multiplier for rows and repeat from **2**, reading rows for stitches.

Calculating stitches for sideways knitted bands

The calculation for the number of stitches required for sideways knitted bands can be made from the stitch and row ratio. Reduce the ratio to its nearest, lowest common denominator, so 16sts and 20rs would be 4 to 5. For every 5rs pick up 4sts. Where the total number of rows is known, multiply it by the fraction 4/5 for the total number of stitches to be picked up. Now check by multiplying the measurement by the stitches for 1cm. Extra stitches are added for the seam and to accommodate a 'V'. Please deal with the neckbands in the patterns in your favourite way. Only essential information is given here.

There is a third expression which I deal with separately in Chapter 10 – bias knitting.

FIVE

The emergence of symbols

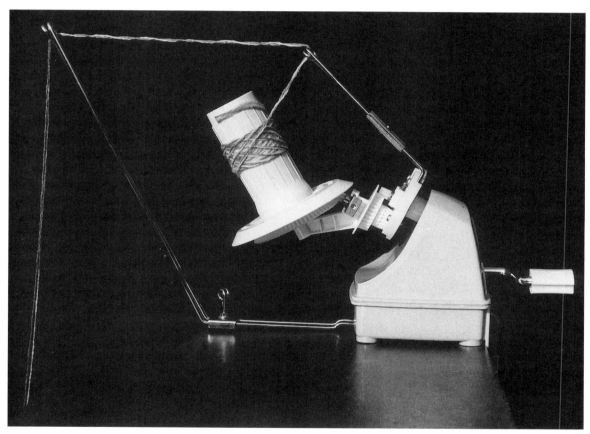

Fig 46
Ball winder and twister

A symbol in knitting is a concise representation of a structural part, a technique or process in the creation of the fabric. Symbols for stitch patterns are arranged in chart form so that a single image can be impressed on the eye, an interpretation done by the mind and communicated to the hand, much more quickly than it would take to read and digest the meaning from conventional writing. Moreover,

the knitter can see the operation clearly, both in total and in stages.

In *Cross Stitch Patterns* (Batsford, 1977) Irmgard Gierl says that as early as 1597 the first pattern book for cross stitches was published in Nurem-

Fig 47
A dragon altered and adapted from Cross Stitch
Patterns *by Irmgard Gierl*

berg. In England it had reached its twelfth edition
by 1640 under the title of *The Needle's Excellency*. In
many instances we know that embroidery provided an inspiration for colour knitting and indeed
for early damask knitting where the raised purl
stitches formed the pattern. Cross stitches are very
easy to translate into knitting; a cross equals one
stitch in the trimming colour. The blank represents
the background. It is as simple as that, although the
translation in knitting may in some instances show
a more squat image.

Richard Rutt writes that between 1748 and
1787, there appeared in Germany a small group of
publications for needlework and knitting, which
failed to discriminate between the two crafts. One of
those books, *New and Useful Knitting Patterns* by
Susanne Dorothea Rieglin, was also published in
Nuremberg. This book, like a work by Schmid, who
published in Augsburg, contained charts but no
text. Recently I bought in a second-hand bookshop

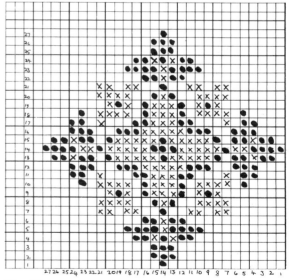

Fig 48
A chart for Berlin work (Mrs Leach, 1886)

a tattered German needlework book called *Kunst
Stricken (Art Knitting)* which I can date *c*.1920–
22. The publisher is Otto Beyer of Leipzig. Most of

61

the lace patterns are both written and in chart form. The symbols used in Burda's collection of knitting patterns are virtually identical.

A modern lace knitter Marianne Kinzel, an Austrian who came to live in Britain, writes about the background to the exquisite lace knitting in Europe, in the introduction to her first book, *Modern Lace Knitting* (Dover 1972). Between the two World Wars there was a revival of the fine lace knitting of the eighteenth and nineteenth centuries in Austria and Germany. Germany has a very long tradition of chart and symbol usage in knitting, probably the longest of any in Europe, and now virtually all the knitting publications which come to Britain from Holland, Italy and France, as well as from Germany, feature garment and stitch patterns in chart form. Until recently, the symbols used did not appear to be from a generally accepted system. However, it is becoming obvious that the Japanese system is now being favoured more than any other.

The use of symbols in Britain

As early as 1842, Mrs Gaugain, in *The Lady's Assistant* (Vol. 2), carried charted designs which were recommended for knitting, crochet or cross stitch. At this early stage, the thought had not occurred that the grid could be of different proportions for the three needlecrafts. Colour knitting was indeed done on small articles and accessories, apparently as a substitute for embroidery.

It is interesting to note that several of Mrs Gaugain's abbreviations were part pictogram and were therefore moving in the direction of symbols. The letter 'A' was for knitting three stitches together. The inverted letter A was for purling three together. 'T' was for taking in or narrowing (decreasing) and the inverted 'T' for purling two together (see Richard Rutt, p. 112).

I have no British patterns in my collection which feature symbols and charts specifically for hand knitting until Marjory Tillotson's from the early 1930s. In the 1880s, however, knitting machines with a jacquard mechanism began to appear in Britain. The jacquard card is in itself a symbol chart presentation which is used in the selection of needles for the pattern in knitting. Issues of *The Knitters' Circular and Monthly Record* from the early

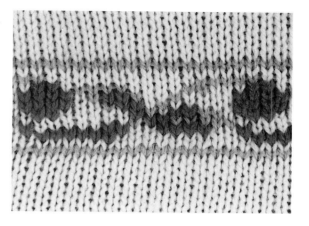

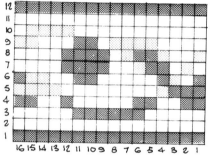

Fig 49a and b
A photograph and chart showing a pattern recommended for knitting by Mrs Gaugain in 1842

1890s frequently carried charts to show colour knitting in jacquard. The first chart I have illustrating three colours in a row (for tartan socks) is from an issue dated October 1895, where crosses, dots and shading are used to represent the three colours. This type of symbolic representation is employed today to show different colours in Fair Isle knitting by hand or by machine. In the 1890s, square gridded graph paper was used and seems to have been readily available.

One might have expected charts to appear when Fair Isle and colour knitting patterns became popular in the 1930s, but although Fair Isle charts were not unknown, British hand knitters seemed quite content with the names of colours abbreviated to one letter. In branded patterns, instructions for Fair Isle were often columns long, though many magazines carried little sketch drawings of the garments annotated with a few measurements.

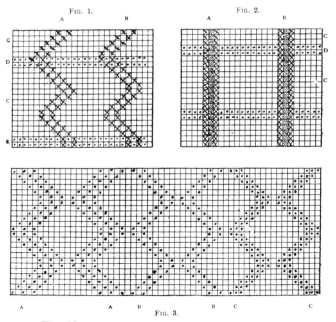

Fig 50

Charts for a 'tartan designing machine' (Knitter's Circular and Monthly Record, *October 1895*)

One such magazine is *Woman's Weekly*, which continues the tradition through to this day. Several freelance writers (as distinct from those sponsored by yarn companies) were in their books carrying charts for Fair Isle, and were experimenting with symbols by the end of the decade.

1930s writers and symbols

Marjory Tillotson's work on symbols and charts is more important than that of Mary Thomas, simply because there is an obvious connection between Marjory Tillotson's system and that of the modern Japanese. In *Modern Needlecraft* (1932), Marjory Tillotson's chart of the 'Falling Leaf lace pattern' for a shawl could easily be the modern Japanese one, but for two main differences. The cross symbol for sl 1, k 2 tog, psso, would be replaced by the arrow head flanked by the leaning stroke in the modern chart. Moreover, the Japanese system would include the purl row as a line of vertical strokes. This brings us to an obvious difficulty that Marjory Tillotson must have recognized and has troubled every writer concerned with promoting symbols.

Tessa Lorant, a hand and machine knitter, offers her own symbol system to hand knitters in her *Collection of Knitted Lace Edgings* (Thorn, 1981). She explains the problem very succinctly: 'Charts do present a difficulty in flat knitting and this is perhaps the reason why they have almost disappeared from modern knitting books written in English.' Tessa Lorant also makes the valuable point that charted patterns avoid the mistakes often found in their written equivalent. If there are mistakes in the charted patterns, they are quickly identified.

Despite this advantage there is one problem with charting. Flat knitting with two needles, as Tessa Lorant explains, involves plain and purl rows. How do you represent purl rows? Marjory Tillotson left them out altogether in her lace patterns, giving only odd numbers for the knit row. In her chart for a lace edging, the purl stitches alternating with the knit are represented, as the Japanese would represent them, by a horizontal bar. To those who object to the modern Japanese influence in knitting, it can be argued convincingly that the British were the first to use many of the symbols which found their way into the Japanese system. Here is yet another case of an innovative approach which the British failed to develop for themselves. (The most ironic example in knitting is the modern domestic machine itself.)

Marjory Tillotson was, however, inconsistent in her approach. In her chart for heel stitches, for example, stocking stitch is represented by one row of vertical strokes and one row of horizontal strokes, which is the modern Japanese way of showing garter stitch. In her representation of a stocking-stitch sample, however, Marjory Tillotson shows only the right side of the fabric by using the vertical stroke for knit stitches, a practice followed by the Japanese for all hand-knitting stitches. In machine knitting, charts are used for the side of the fabric facing the knitter, and that is why the horizontal bars for purl are the background. When the background to a stitch pattern is understood to be either knit or purl the Japanese often leave it blank or sometimes put a few strokes in a corner of a large chart. Since most lace patterns are symmetrical, these charts can be used by both hand and machine knitters. Where the pattern is asymmetri-

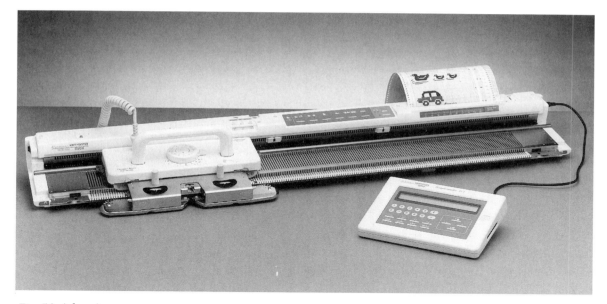

Fig 51 *(above)*
Knitmaster 580 and Designmaster. Patterns on design sheets can be stored by the computer

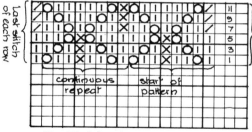

Fig 52 *(above)*
Marjory Tillotson's chart (1932) for falling leaf lace

Fig 53 *(below)*
*Modern Japanese charts for falling leaf lace.
Left: hand-knitted; centre: machine-knitted;
right: hand- and machine-knitted*

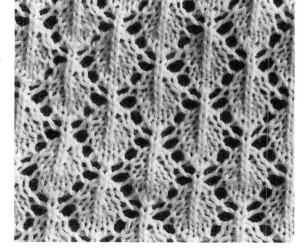

Fig 54 *(above)*
Falling leaf lace worked on a knitting machine

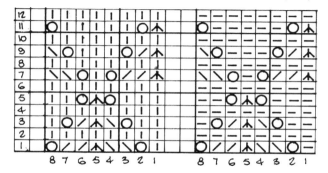

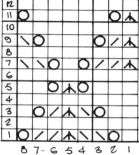

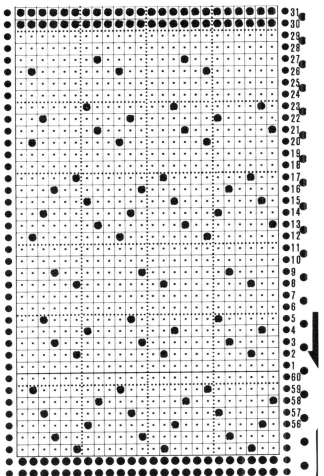

Fig 55
Punchcard for fig 54

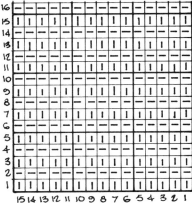

Fig 56
Chart for stocking stitch on a heel (Marjory Tillotson, 1932) and garter stitch (Japanese)

ing her earlier system, she uses a different one in her book. In one way it was backward looking, yet in another it looked forward to the Japanese pictogram method for choosing symbols. She changed the vertical and horizontal bars to a horseshoe loop for knit and a saucer ellipse for purl. The reasoning is clear – each looked like the stitch it was intended to represent. The Japanese did not follow suit, for their experience of ideogram and pictogram characters in their language told them that economical strokes were best for eye impact. They were right.

Marjory Tillotson's change of approach sent other writers off in various directions. Catherine

cal, machine knitters will see the pattern in reverse on the knit side. As this happens when working intarsia and odd-stitch cables, it is not an unknown situation for those not used to using diagrams and so doesn't cause too many headaches. In cable and lace patterns, once the symbol system is understood, the pattern can be turned around on the chart before beginning to knit, thus ensuring a faithful copy of the hand-knit version is made, if that is what is wanted.

One wonders what happened to change Marjory Tillotson's approach in the two years between the publication of *Modern Needlecraft* (1932) and her *Complete Knitting Book* (1934). Instead of develop-

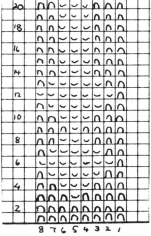

Fig 57
Solid pattern border (Marjory Tillotson, 1934). Loop = knit, ellipse = purl

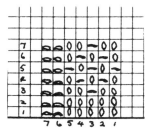

Fig 58
*Fancy rib (Catherine Franks, 1939). Note the two
symbols for purl*

Franks' system in *The Pictorial Guide to Modern
Home Knitting* (1939) is a little confusing, but at
least her symbols resemble knit and purl stitches.
Although Catherine Franks used square-gridded
graph paper, she did observe: 'as knitted stitches
are a little shorter than their width, the diagram
will become a little deeper than the knitting will be
when worked.' Mary Thomas's squiggles, blobs
and curls leave one with a decided preference for
her written instructions. She was, however, the
first writer to display stitch patterns on rectangu-
lar-gridded graph paper in her *Book of Knitting
Patterns*. As far as symbols are concerned, these
authors of the 1930s were tackling virtually
unaided a huge communication problem and must
surely earn a place in the history of the craft. Their
efforts taught the lesson that symbols must be both
dramatically simple and hold a visual appeal.
Strangely enough the German Burda system with
its solid squares, triangles and bars across grids,
does not give a graphic pictorial representation of
the pattern, yet its popularity continues with many
German knitters although it is beginning to be
overtaken by the Japanese system. Providing one
reads the key and refers to it in the early stages of
interpretation, any symbolic representation must
be easier to follow than lines and lines of written
instructions.

After the Second World War, Marianne Kinzel's
lace charts used a system which is very close to the
modern Japanese one, including, as it does the
arrow symbol for sl 1, k 2 tog, psso.

No survey of modern hand knitting would be
complete without mention of the monumental
achievement of the American writer Barbara
Walker, whose books of hand-knit stitch patterns
have been a constant inspiration to hand and
machine knitters alike. In her *Charted Knitting
Designs* (1972), Barbara Walker shows for the first
time the representations for cables similar to the
ones the Japanese use. Purl stitches are illustrated
by a background of dots, but the cable twists are
blank and outlined in black, giving a very bold,
graphic impression of the actual pattern. In her
introduction, Barbara Walker offers many reasons
why charted patterns are preferable to the written
text:

> 'A chart does what written out instructions
> cannot do: it shows the knitter something
> resembling a picture of the finished work. This
> can be very useful for learning an unfamiliar
> pattern . . . After learning how to chart
> patterns, you will probably find yourself NOT
> KNITTING your way through a set of written
> out directions, but drawing your way through
> them the first time round.'

Perhaps it was this example, as well as a familiarity
with the world's reception of the Japanese system,
that persuaded the American publishers of *Vogue
Knitting* and *Knitters* to represent stitch patterns on
Japanese-style charts. By any standards, these two
magazines are the most outstanding of their kind in
the English-speaking world. It is also significant
that the famous Italian hand-knit magazine,
Filatura di Crosa, promotes some of the Japanese
symbols in its international issues (but, noticeably,
not in those intended purely for the British market).
Filatura di Crosa deserves mention as the first
international hand-knitting magazine to include
an appreciable number of quality patterns for
machine knitters. The Italians perhaps exert the
most influence of all the Europeans in the area of
knitwear design.

Present-day advocates of symbols in handknitting

In her *Handknitter's Handbook* (1986), a book justly
acclaimed as a worthy successor to Mary Thomas's
Knitting Book, Montse Stanley reflects current
practice and the highly individual systems promoted by authors in Britain when she writes:
'Symbols are far from standard. The best symbols

are those which reflect texture, such as . . .' It is interesting that the examples given are some of the best-known Japanese symbols for lace. The Japanese symbols for lace and purl stitches are also used by Maggie Whiting in *The Progressive Knitter* (Batsford, 1988). It is no coincidence that both these authors are members of the Knitting and Crochet Guild.

Until there is a universally accepted system, it is obvious that some writers will promote their own. It is heartening to read the late Rae Compton's commendation of charts in her *Illustrated Dictionary of Knitting* (Batsford, 1988), a book rich in interesting stitch patterns and techniques. What is puzzling is that even at this late date the symbols Rae Compton uses are her own.

Symbols and the modern machine knitter

Before the Japanese machines appeared on the market, many machine-knitting magazines used basic symbol representations for hand-tooled lace patterns and charts for hand-selected Fair Isle. It would have been equally simple to represent tuck stitches or the needle arrangements for tuck lace in the same way, but no one thought to do so. At that time it was far too easy to get confused when trying to follow a written pattern and hand select the correct needles, particulary during increasing and decreasing. Charts for hand-knit Fair Isle which were adopted by machine knitters, had been previously promoted by Marjory Tillotson.

After the Japanese push-button machines arrived in Britain in the mid-1960s, charts began to appear with instructions for which buttons to press and knobs to turn. The charts in the pattern books for the Brother 585 and 588 went a step further. They showed the Japanese symbol charts for the pattern at the side of the machine instructions. Then the punchcard and electronic machines arrived and there did not seem as much need to give the stitch patterns in Japanese symbols as well as the punchcard and mylar sheet representation. Despite this, a symbol chart did appear in the Knitmaster 321 manual. The Japanese magazines, on the other hand, often gave just the symbol chart, especially for lace, and invited Brother and Knitmaster knitters to produce their own punchcard or mylar sheet interpretations.

With the recent popularity of chunky machines in the English-speaking world, however, the symbol system is now being used more widely to represent hand-tooled stitch patterns. Certainly I found it necessary to print the symbol charts and use the symbols for patterns in my two-volume work *Handtooling for the Chunky Machine* and I found it impossible to design mosaic, slip and tuck stitches without charting the patterns first. I am by no means the only machine-knit writer to use symbols; most of my colleagues use the Japanese system easily and naturally.

In recent years many machine knitters have had access to imported Japanese magazines, and it has become apparent just how easy it is to communicate stitch patterns by an internationally accepted code of symbols. Because the garment diagrams can be 'read' as well, we have found we can follow and knit Japanese language patterns without any understanding of the Japanese characters and printed text.

Abbreviations

ff – fully fashioned, sts – stitches, HK – hand knitting, MK – machine knitting NWP – non-working position, WP – working position, tog – together, sl – slip, psso – pass slipped stitch over, ssk – slip, slip, knit, tbl – through back of loop, k – knit, rs – (in patterns) rows, WY – waste yarn, st st – stocking stitch, T – tension (MK).

Explanation of Japanese symbols

Below are some of the most commonly-used symbols:

ᵒᵒᵒᵒ Cast on by chain.

ᴜᴜ Cast on by over-cast or e-wrap.

●●●● Cast off or bind off.

| Knit stitch.

— Purl stitch.

Ɋ Twisted stitch.

Ɣ Increase with lean to right. Increase is made by picking up the head of the stitch below at left.

⅂ Increase with lean to left. Increase is made by picking up the head of the stitch below at right.

✕ Cross right stitch over left. Right stitch at front.

✕ Cross left stitch over right. Left stitch at front.

ᐯ Multiple increase into same stitch. Example has 3 sts made from 1. When the V symbol is inverted the 3 are decreased to 1 again. Use for bobbles and popcorns.

⩜ Slip stitch with slip bar on knit side.

ᐯ Slip stitch with slip bar on purl side.

∩ Raised stitch made by dropping stitch and unravelling the number of rows indicated. Pick up stitch and unravelled bars and knit them all off into one new stitch.

Tuck stitch. Loops are held for the number of rows indicated and then knitted off.

⫍⫎ Manual pull up of stitch from 5 rows below and worked on the purl side. Symbol narrower than for tuck.

ℛ Twisted pick up or tuck stitch.

✕ Left stitch is crossed and pulled over right hand stitch. In HK process is worked on the left needle and transferred to the right.

✕ Right stitch is crossed and pulled over left stitch. In HK move 2 stitches first to right needle. In MK transfer stitch underneath first. Cross 2nd stitch through middle of first with double-eyed bodkin.

⌣ MK only – needle at NWP as in tuck lace.

Cables

⚹ 2 over 2. Right on top, left underneath.

⚹ 2 over 2. Left on top, right underneath.

⚹ 3 over 3. Right on top, left underneath.

⚹ 3 over 3. Left on top, right underneath.

Lace

◯ Lace hole made by over. In HK. MK empty needle in WP after transfer. Yarn over needle in first row.

╲ Stitch leaning to left.

╱ Stitch leaning to right.

⤨ HK – knit 2 tog (right lean). MK – transfer left stitch on to right needle.

⤩ HK – sl 1, k 1, psso, or ssk or k 2 tog tbl (left lean). MK – transfer right stitch on to left needle.

⋏ HK – sl 2 tog knitwise, k 1, psso. MK – transfer stitch right of centre on to centre needle at left. Transfer stitch left of centre on to centre needle at right (3 stitches on centre needle).

⋋ HK – sl 1, k 2 tog, psso. MK – lift centre stitch on to a single transfer tool. Move the left stitch and then the right one on to the centre needle before replacing the original stitch (manual only).

⋌ HK – k 3 tog. MK – lift centre stitch on to a single transfer tool. Move stitch at right on to centre needle. Replace centre stitch. Transfer stitch on left on to centre needle (manual only).

Note on new symbols

In Japanese magazines diagrams illustrating new symbols are printed to show their relationship to newly-invented stitch patterns or techniques. Some of these additional symbols pass into common usage. A fully comprehensive selection for hand knitting is obtainable from Nihon Vogue. The latest Japanese magazines for both hand and machine knitting include new additons as well as the long-established symbols in the charts which accompany the patterns.

Symbols for colour knitting

The symbols used for colour knitting are diverse and follow no prescribed pattern. On Mrs Gaugain's charts of 1842 the following representations were used: blank for the background and pale

Fig 59a and b
Mosaic pattern. Left: hand-knitted using garter slip stitch; right: machine-knitted using stocking slip stitch

and dark filled-in squares for the second and third colours. Today the symbols used are sometimes based on Mrs Gaugain's representations and at others the x-symbol is used for the second colour and blank for the background. Strongly marked dots, circles, diagonal strokes and triangles are used to represent more than two colours in multi-coloured Fair Isle, intarsia or jacquard knitting. When there are numerous changes of background and trimming colours, an alphabetical code is employed alongside a simple two-colour chart, or else a full pictorial representation is given in colour. I usually write the letter representing the trimming colour at the left and the letter for the background at the right, using the right-hand-side of the chart only. This is to remind me – as a machine knitter – of the order in the yarn feed. Note that strongly marked circles indicate the second or trimming

colour in a punchcard representation for Fair Isle. They should present no problem to a hand-knitter wishing to interpret in two-colour work. Please remember that the standard punchcard has a 24st repeat, so within its boundaries you can have stitch bases of 2, 3, 4, 6, 8, and 12.

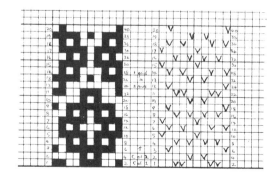

Fig 60
Image and working charts for fig 59

69

Note on the proportions of stitch-related graph paper

A stitch/row ratio is determined by dividing the rows per 10cm (4in) by the stitches. Thus, 25sts and 25rs requires a graph paper grid of 1:1, *i.e.* square, whereas 29sts and 34rs requires a slightly rectangular one of 1:1.2, the longer lines being the horizontal representation of a stitch's width. Packs of various grids are available from many knit shops. The stitch-related graph paper widely advertised for machine knitters has a grid of around 1:1.3. It is often easier, though, for an author to use square gridded graph paper with a caution to readers that the shape of the pattern on the paper may not have the same proportions as that of its knitted version. Certainly punchcards, but not the mylar sheets for the electronic machines, have a square grid, and therefore this problem is not unfamiliar to machine knitters. In this book, then, I have tried to use charts with the most appropriate grid. Charts from other sources are represented in the grid ratio of their original form.

SIX

Exploring and mixing stitch patterns

Fig 61

Knitmaster 155 – chunky machine with ribber

During the eighteenth and nineteenth centuries, framework knitters took their lace samplers round to prospective employers as testimony to their ability. A collection of these can be seen at the Ruddington Framework Museum near Nottingham. There is also an interesting lined, cut and sewn waistcoat with an intriguing transfer pattern in the Victoria and Albert Museum, London. The garment has been worked either on a ribbing frame in a fine, full needle rib, which has a stocking stitch appearance, or on a single bed frame, where the stitches in stocking stitch have been transferred against the grain to form eyelets and not faggots. A century later, the Victorian lady knitted her lace samplers in white wool, silk or cotton, and such hand-knitted samplers are now collectors' items.

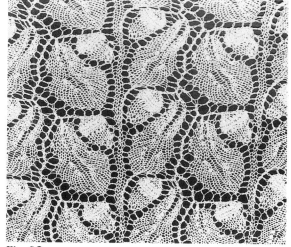

Fig 62

Victorian hand-knitted lace

Fig 63
Pillowcases and table cloths adorned with lace edgings (Clara Sedgwick)

Fig 64
Cover of Needlecraft Practical Journal, *c.1900*

Fig 65
Pages from Mary Capstick's exercise book

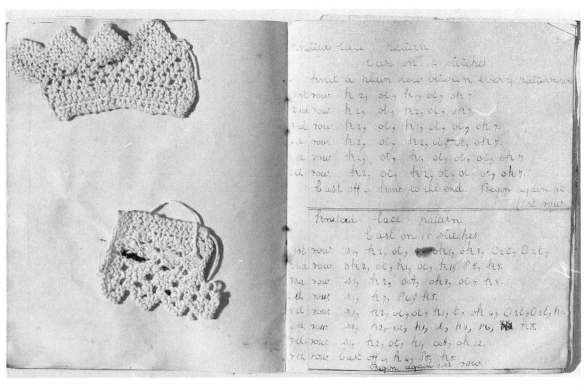

Some pieces are quite exquisite, representing a high point of the knitter's art. Many of the pieces were no doubt patterns which the knitter would find in needlecraft publications. Others must have been the invention of the knitter and passed around friends and neighbours before going into general circulation. Some of the teachers' manuals included patterns for interesting stitches which were no doubt dictated to the children.

I have been kindly lent an exercise book of knitted lace patterns belonging to 'Mary Capstick, Standard 6'. The name is a Yorkshire Dales one, but the village and the school are unknown. From the faded copperplate writing, the terms used and the little cotton samples pinned to the pages with now rusty pins, the book seems to date from the end of the nineteenth century. The patterns are similar to the ones I have seen Clara Sedgwick knit, but Mary Capstick's patterns are, in the main, very simple and like the garter stitch edgings in several teachers' manuals. A child who could knit lace edgings for tablecloths and pillowcases had a useful accomplishment indeed. By the turn of the century, thousands of these patterns were in circulation. All are anonymous, and no one seems to know who invented them.

Collections of hand-knit stitch patterns continue to pour off the presses. In Britain the format hasn't changed in a hundred years. All are written, and only those from Europe, the USA, Japan and those for machine knitters are in diagrammatic form. As far as hand knitters are concerned, I cannot think of one publication, except Barbara Walker's *Charted Stitch Patterns*, where it is put to the knitter that he or she might invent original stitch patterns (though Rae Compton does suggest in her last book that if knitters alter existing patterns, new ones might emerge). The implication is that there are plenty already in circulation, and that it is the knitter's function to copy and not invent. It seems that hand knitters have never questioned this attitude. My view is that the feminist movement should have targeted British hand knitting long ago, not to destroy but to reform.

British machine knitters, on the other hand, are used to altering existing stitch patterns as well as inventing their own. British machine knitters are now insisting that the new computerized machines

Fig 66
Lace sampler – stitches from Brother 930–950 built-in patterns

should offer plenty of scope for inventing stitch patterns. A few years ago the Brother 950 machine was chosen by Jones and Brother UK in preference to the 930, which other countries accepted but which had not as much facility for original pattern-making as the 950. The built-in patterns in both the 930 and 950 are used, and indeed the lace ones are beautiful, but we reserve the right to make our own surface patterns as well. The new software now offers unlimited scope on both the 930 and the 950.

It is doubtful whether a machine which makes the creation of personalized stitch patterns difficult would be a success on the British market. The reason why machine knitters differ from their hand-knitting counterparts is not that they are 'different' people, as some authorities have suggested, but that machine knitters are already used

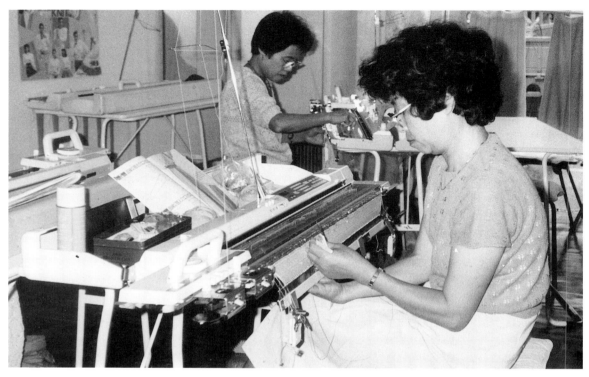

Fig 67
A Japanese student using the Brother 930 electronic machine

to working from diagrams and have had a liberal education at the hands of the Japanese. It is unlikely that the following comment from Barbara Walker's *Charted Knitting Patterns* could have been written by a contemporary British hand-knitting authority:

> 'A system of charting makes it much easier for anyone to be a designer of knitting patterns . . . Charting is an extremely valuable aid to the knitter who wishes to do her own garment designing and that means almost everyone sooner or later.'

Traditionally, lace patterns have been among the first to be translated into symbols. Today, lace suffers from neglect due to the current passion for colour. Indeed, we have almost forgotten how to appreciate stitch texture and space in monochromatic knitting. Moreover, lace tends to look best on a sleeveless or fitted sleeve top, and the latter shape is just fighting its way back into the fashion scene. In the past, I have hand knitted lace and translated the pattern to a punchcard. Lace is not easy to design from cold, but by studying lace pattern charts and then getting to grips with the moves, understanding finally dawns. Then it is possible to start playing around with the symbols, re-arranging them on the charts. Machine knitters, please study my book *Techniques in Machine Knitting* (Batsford, 1983) for a more detailed explanation of how to transfer lace patterns from symbols to punchcards and mylar sheets.

The symbol chart approach is quite different from the way hand-knit lace patterns were invented in the past, at least as far as Britain is concerned, but it certainly works for us now and is, moreover, a system which young people can understand. It is also possible to chart garter and purl damask stitch patterns to use with the garter carriage and I have worked out Aran patterns to handtool. When I go to hand knitting, I find the skills immediately transferable. The stitch pattern areas I have mentioned, plus mosaics, cables and lacy ribs, are interchangeable between the two knitting crafts. We do not count Fair Isle and intarsia (see Chapter 7) because they are stocking-stitch based patterns.

The best way to begin is to hand knit or hand tool on the machine using patterns from charts or written instructions. If you cannot translate the written pattern directly into chart form, then it is better to hand knit it first to help understanding.

Lace

In her exercise book, Mary Capstick uses 'seam' as the old word for purl which, according to Richard Rutt, dates back to 1655. The letter 'o' in her patterns was commonly used throughout the nineteenth and early twentieth centuries to mean 'yarn over'. Indeed it still is today – see the Japanese symbol charts. As I said in the previous chapter, the letter 't' was Mrs Gaugain's abbreviation for take in or narrow. The question is: What does 'narrow' mean? Is it k 2 tog, or k 1, sl 1, psso? Perhaps 'narrow' could be k 2 tog tbl, which gives a slightly twisted version of k 1, sl 1, psso. I tried both these suggestions but they looked decidedly wrong, even though the decreases were following the directional line of the holes. Then I discovered that as virtually all the edgings in the exercise book are in garter stitch, one needs only to use k 2 tog for the narrowings. The appearance is slightly chunky, like crochet, but the shapings look correct, no matter whether the line of holes leans to the right or to the left. I then went through my Victorian and early twentieth-century collection and found that in every example of garter stitch lace, 'narrow' meant k 2 tog. These garter stitch edgings are very easy to do and this is why they were given to children to knit. Moreover they lie flat and firm, and are reversible, and so perfectly suited as edgings for pillowcases, table and tray cloths, etc. Today they look beautiful adorning the neckline and sleeves of a summer top. The edgings cannot be done automatically in their garter stitch form on the modern machine, but they can be hand tooled. Hand-knitted garter-stitch edgings co-ordinate well with machine-knit fabric. We can punch or mark stocking-stitch versions to be knitted automatically on the knitting machine. In some cases, though, it is easier to hand tool.

When I had knitted the samples, I put each pattern on a symbol chart. Please remember that you are looking at the right side of the pattern when you study a chart, and even though you knit on every row in garter stitch, the alternate rows are represented as purl. That is indeed what they are when you study garter stitch on its right side.

Mary Capstick's two garter-stitch edgings are worked as follows:

Number One
1st row: k2, ot, k1, ot, ok7.
2nd row: k2, ot, k2, ot, ok7.
3rd row: k2, ot, k1, ot, ot, ok7.
4th row: k2, ot, k2, ot, ot, ok7.
5th row: k2, ot, k1, ot, ot, ot, ok7.
6th row: k2, ot, k2, ot, ot, ot, ok7.
Cast off 6. Knit to end. Begin again at the first row.

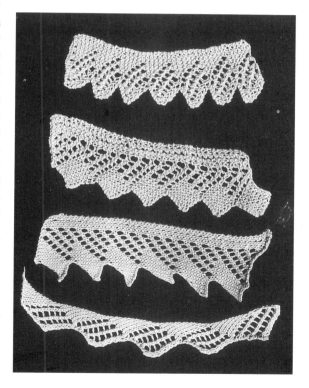

Fig 68
Two of Mary Capstick's edgings. Top: *hand-knitted garter stitch;* bottom: *machine-knitted stocking stitch*

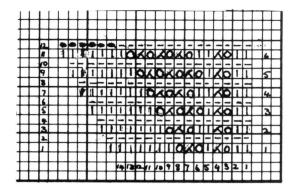

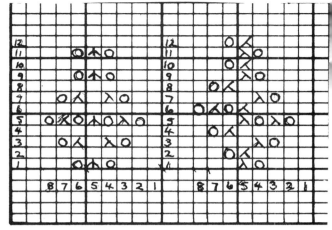

Fig 70
Festoon lace. Left: fashion; *right:* simple or plain

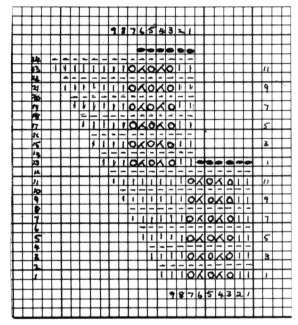

Fig 69
Charts for Fig 68. Top: *no. 1;* bottom: *no. 2*

Once I had knitted and charted this one, I could chart the other patterns in the exercise book before knitting and trying them out. Moreover, I could see how to alter and/or enlarge the patterns and how to change them to stocking stitch versions for the machine. I hand knitted all the edgings first in soft 4-ply cotton on cone using 3mm needles.

On the machine, you could try number 1 as a hand-tooled version and move the 7sts with a 7-eyed transfer tool. To interpret the ot instructions precisely, i.e. the k2 tog symbol with the lean away from the lace hole, you would have to move the stitch from its needle, deposit the transferred stitch

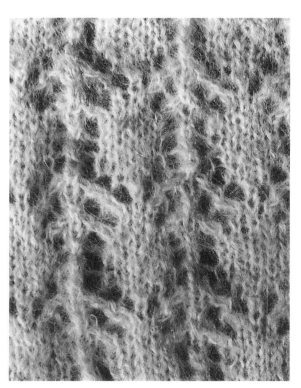

Fig 71
Festoon lace (fashion), hand-knitted in mohair

and then replace the original one. Instead I take the easy way and merely bring up an empty needle at the edge. This produces an attractive firm side. It is

76

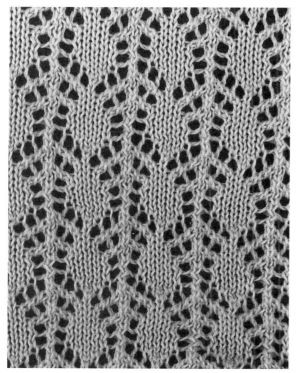

Fig 72
Festoon lace (simple), machine-knitted in 4-ply cotton on Knitmaster 560

not worth punching a card, since you can almost hand tool a collar or sleeve edging in the time it takes for marking or punching. So, here is an original machine-knit lace inspired by a hand-knit one, which came in the first place from a most unlikely source.

Number Two
This pattern looks like a simple garter-stitch version of a godmother lace edging. In contrast to number one, the peaks are in lace and not in garter stitch. It was very quick to knit by hand. Either would make a beautiful collar for a lace blouse. Cast on 9 stitches.

    1st row: k2, ot, ot, ok3.
    2nd and every alt. row: knit plain.
    3rd row: k2, ot, ot, ok4.
    5th row: k2, ot, ot, ok5.
    7th row: k2, ot, ot, ok6.
    9th row: k2, ot, ot, ok7.

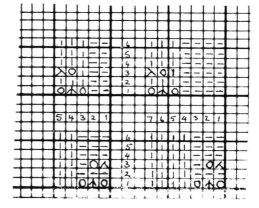

Fig 73
Charts for lacy rib variations. Top: *hand-knit;* bottom: *machine-knit*

11th row: k2, ot, ot, ok8.
12th row: Knit to end. At beginning of second and all following repeat sequences, cast off 6 stitches.

The instructions for row 12 are mine as I found the original pattern was wrong here. We were instructed to cast off 6 at the beginning of the 12th row but the chart showed up the mistake clearly. The cast-off stitches had to be over the lace holes in row 1, and not over the solid garter stitch as in number one. The chart also revealed how clever, yet how deceptively simple, this pattern is. In actual fact it is constructed on the bias and you can see this clearly when you hand tool on the machine, for the edging moves 6 needles along the bed every sequence. However, because the bias pulls in both directions, the one corrects the other in the hand-knit piece, though the k2 tog bias is stronger than the 'o' increase. The garter stitch knitting appears straight and the lace diamonds follow an attractive diagonal. I have illustrated two sequences on the charted hand-knit version. It would not be easy to put this one on to a punchcard or mylar sheet. It proved even quicker to hand tool than number one. If you wish, add more plain stitches to make the edging deeper.

Lacy rib pattern with mock cable

A short time ago, I sampled my own two versions of a well-known hand-knit stitch pattern with the

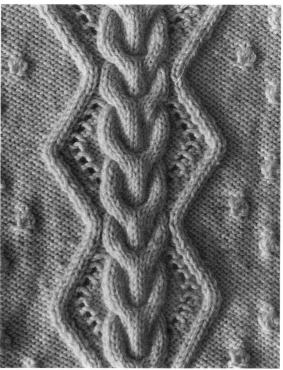

Fig 74
A slipover made up to show the reverse side of lacy mock cable rib

Fig 75
Close-up of Aran lattice pattern with popcorns (hand-knitted by Margaret Rhodes)

intention of choosing one of them to hand knit into a simple slipover. I could not really decide, so I ended up knitting the top with one side in one version and the other in the alternative, illustrated on page 77 and above. The version with four separating stitches has a gauge of 23sts and 24rs per 10cm (4in), while the one with two separating stitches has 22sts and 24rs per 10cm (4in) the latter being the more lacy. Most people who know the pattern will recall that there are usually 3 separating stitches. It was quite a surprise to see what the difference of 2 stitches did to the main mock cable pattern. This pattern, then, illustrates very well how to begin designing your own stitch patterns, particularly if you haven't the confidence to launch into something entirely new at the onset. The garment pattern at the end of the chapter is given in the stitch pattern *I* prefer, but the choice is yours.

The pattern can be hand tooled very quickly on a chunky machine with ribber. I have turned the

setting round so that you can transfer the stitches on the main bed rather than on the ribber. Please note that the seven flanking stitches at each side are plain stocking stitch. These make the garment easy to seam up. The yarn is Aran weight and the stitch pattern makes a lovely crunchy fabric whichever version you choose.

Materials: 575g Aran wool.
Needles: 3.75mm (US 5) for ribs, 4.5mm (US 7) for pattern.
Size: Bust 100cm (40in). Length 60cm (24in).
Tension/gauge: 22sts, 24rs per 10cm (4in), swatch slightly stretched.
Directions:
1. MK: See Fig 72 for reversed pattern. Read 7sts at beginning and end as purl.
2. ALL: Mark armhole edges with waste yarn.
3. Hold shoulder sts on WY before grafting. Use mattress stitch for side seams.

Fig 76a
Ladies' lacy mock cable rib slipover

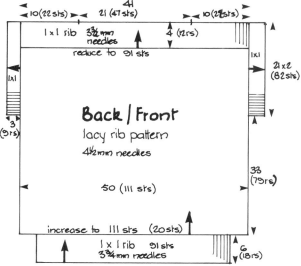

Fig 76b
Ladies' lacy mock cable rib slipover – charts.
Left: *main pattern;* right: *right and left edges*

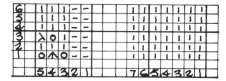

Fig 76c
Ladies' lacy mock cable rib slipover – working diagram

Garter, purl and knit stitch variations

In the Victoria and Albert Museum, London, there is a petticoat, thought to have been worked in Holland, which is a fine example of a type of knitting popular in the seventeenth and eighteenth centuries. The surface pattern, a landscape of animals and foliage after the manner of Jacobean embroidery, is self-coloured, composed of textures provided by purl and plain arrangements. These include purl (reversed stocking stitch) and moss stitch on a mainly stocking stitch background. The fabric appears to have been beautifully and evenly knitted, but some of the details do not emerge clearly because of the kind of pattern chosen. Another garment, and one of the most beautiful knitted in plain and purl arrangements, is the vest said to have been worn by Charles I at his execution. Richard Rutt explains succinctly the advantages and disadvantages of this type of stitch pattern, which he appropriately calls damask (others have called it figured or embossed) in *A History of Handknitting*. The basic principle is that the purled areas should stand out in relief from the plain knitted background, rather like the pattern on a damask weave. In knitting, this does not happen uniformly, and the sides of a purl shape sink into the background, often leading to loss of clarity. Plain areas on purl are better, while moss stitch and double moss stitch can be the most successful of all. The choice of yarn is of crucial importance. It needs to be crisp and firm to show off the stitchery.

Damask knitting, including moss stitch variants, is used most effectively as low relief to contrast with sculptured effects provided by cabling and Aran patterns. The old gansey knitters who produced the fishermen's sweaters and jerseys were experts at

79

Fig 77
Charles I's vest

1 Teaching hand knitting at the Nihon Vogue Technological Institute of Knitting

2 Regency and Victorian pinballs and cushions (York)

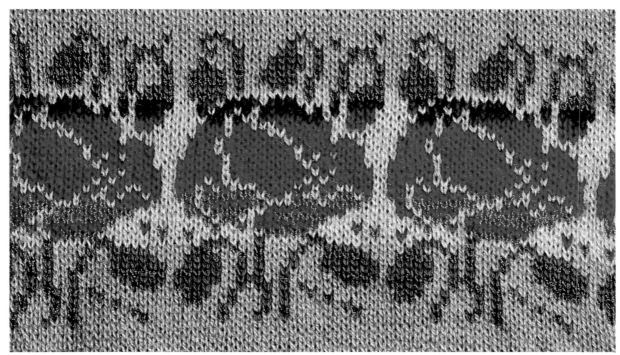

3 Poppies

4 The alternative

5 Damask garter stitch gansey

6 Paton's carnations

7 Carnation jacket

8 Kaffe Fassett's Chinese Roses Jacket (Rowan)

9 Intarsia butterfly sweater

10 Sweater in Aran trellis lace popcorns

11 Full circular yoke

12 Close-up of chunky yoke

13 Full circular yoked sweater

14 Bias knitted mohair top

Fig 78
*Damask garter stitch. When the garment was made
up this side became the inside*

this. With the arrival of the Brother garter carriage
for machine knitters, there is now greater opportunity to explore this genre of stitchery and to
experiment with different combinations of plains
and purls to find out which afford the greatest
contrast and make the most pleasing eye appeal.
The garter carriage proceeds slowly but it can be set
for so many rows and left to get on with the
knitting. It will take up to a soft Aran weight of yarn
easily, and you can move the tension dial to three
points beyond the 10. Patterns designed in a
diagonal direction are often very effective. Blocks
separated by garter stitch bands can be pleasing
while the most successful have bold outlines and a
mixture of patterning bases like the Charles I vest.
In the pattern I designed for this book (Fig 80a), I
found the reverse side to be the more impressive,
but the choice is yours. If you, as a machine knitter,
have no Brother machine and garter carriage,

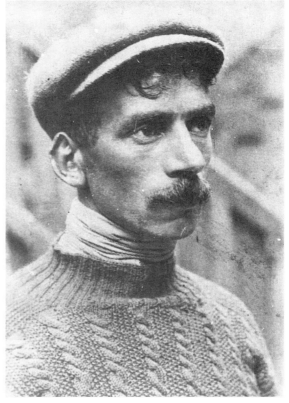

Fig 79
Unknown fisherman wearing his gansey

81

substitute a suitable tuck stitch which has a similar textured appearance, otherwise sample in handknitting.

The charts used for these types of design must be the easiest of all to follow and, indeed, one occasionally sees charts in hand-knitting books for damask knitting. Gladys Thompson used them in her celebrated *Jerseys, Guernseys and Arans*, which must be a main source of inspiration, but I find her tiny framed black and white squares trying on the eye. My instinct is to transfer them to the easily read vertical and horizontal strokes of the Japanese symbol chart. On the punchcard or mylar sheet the marks represent knit stitches on the side facing the knitter. Of course, in this kind of work either side can be the right side. Most of the cards are easily marked. However, when cables are incorporated

with damask knitting some thought needs to be given to the marks on the card. The cables are represented by purl stitches facing the knitter – plain on the card – and only up to 2 over 2 sts can be crossed without the use of a separate piece of yarn.

The following damask garter-stitch gansey is one I have designed. It can be worked either by hand or on a machine:

Materials: 400g DK (US worsted) acrylic.
Machine: Brother punchcard or electronic with garter carriage.
Needles: 3.25mm (US 5) for rib, 4mm (US 6) for pattern.
Size: Bust 96cm (38in). Length 56cm (22½in). Sleeve length 40cm (16in).
Tension/gauge: 26sts, 33.5rs per 10cm (4in).

Fig 80a
Damask garter stitch gansey

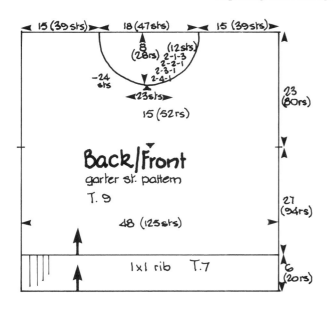

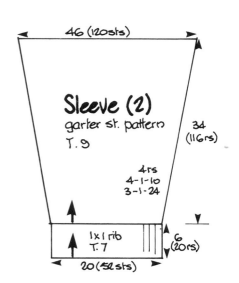

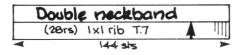

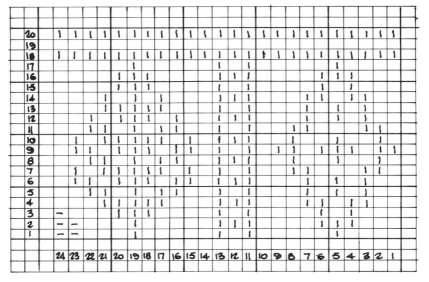

Directions:

1. MK: Interpret vertical strokes as punched holes as marks (electronics). The side facing the knitter is the right side.

2. MK: The neckline is cut and sewn. HK: Note the breakdowns on the front neck.

Fig 80b *(top)*
Damask garter stitch gansey – working diagrams

Fig 80c *(bottom)*
Damask garter stitch gansey – chart

83

The conversion factor

If you want to knit any pattern from this book, or elsewhere, and you cannot get the required tension gauge, you have a choice of alternatives. You can of course re-design the whole pattern from cold and work out a new set of breakdowns, but you must then bear in mind that what you eventually produce may not look the same as the original. This is especially true if you use a yarn other than the one recommended. However people often use yarn other than the one stated in the pattern. Some enjoy mixing their own yarn from a selection of fine weights. If you are interested in yarn mixing, a combined ball winder and yarn twister is a good investment.

Another option is pattern conversion. This is speedy and works well for conversions of patterns within hand or machine knitting or from hand knitting to machine knitting or vice versa. It is especially successful when the gauge differences are small. The example below is for a conversion from a hand-knit pattern to one for a chunky machine:

Hand-knit gauge: 19sts and 26rs per 10cm (4in).

Machine-knit gauge: 20sts and 28rs per 10cm (4in).

The conversion factor is achieved by dividing the gauge you want by the gauge in the given pattern. In the case of the stitches in the example, divide 20 by 19, for rows, divide 28 by 26. Use a calculator.

Answers: For stitches, 1.053; for rows, 1.077. Return to the pattern and multiply all stitch breakdowns by 1.053, and all row breakdowns by 1.077. If you need to alter any measurements it is easier to re-design the pattern.

SEVEN

Colour, design and the dropped shoulder line

When a customer disapproved of William Morris's use of colour in his textiles and wallpaper, Morris replied that there was plenty of mud in the street. However, Morris himself was no example to follow in the matter of colour or even of hygiene in personal dress. According to contemporaries, he was completely careless about his appearance. He had no time to comb his hair and wore the same dingy waistcoat and trousers day in and day out. On the other hand, his output as a designer of beautiful surface patterns was prodigious. Today one wonders sometimes if knitwear designers are giving enough thought to the person for whom their creations are intended. Who will wear a chunky, rainbow-coloured top with a huge intarsia butterfly motif? When and with what can it be worn? The wearing environment must always be considered in advance of the design and planning stage, and the designer too ought to wear his/her own creations. Many do, but there are those who see hand-crafted knitwear as the wearing apparel of others, who may or may not exist in reality. I believe that such a theoretical approach will ensure the demise of knitting as a popular garment-making craft. Knitwear has won its fight to be regarded as an art-form but there is a real danger that its sartorial function is being forgotten. There are too many admiring spectators and not enough knitters and wearers.

At present, garments that strike the eye as beautiful in colour and design, appear to have a good chance of success with the general public. There is also a general appreciation of the value of harmonious colour, pleasing texture and pattern. Kaffe Fassett's great achievement is that he has

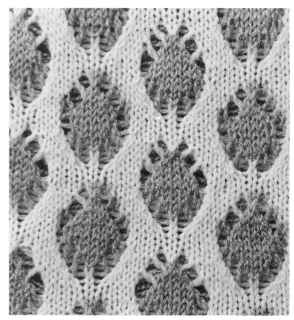

Fig 81
Lace with Fair Isle (Electronic Knitting, *Kinder*)

released for our enjoyment the myriad hues locked within our grey environment. I usually use my most colourful and striking patterns in jackets. For one thing, jackets are more voluminous and make better canvases than sweaters. They can be slipped on and off as the occasion arises. One can wear a jacket with a skirt or trousers and the accompanying garments can be in subdued colours to provide a good foil for the jacket worn on top. Since a jacket is exposed to view, one can test its appeal in the eyes of the public, and the local supermarket is, I've found, a good place to launch a new design!

Colour knitting: some historical facts

Colour knitting in stranded stocking stitch, or Fair Isle as we imprecisely call it, dates to AD 600–800, and fragments were first discovered in Egypt. By the twelfth century, quite complicated geometric patterns were being worked on socks and other objects. Some beautiful and quite sophisticated colour knitting was produced in Spain before 1500. Moreover, by the thirteenth to fourteenth centuries, a type of single-motif knitting had made its appearance in Egypt and Europe. This is best described as halfway between stranding and true intarsia which came much later. Stranded stocking stitch was predominant in colour knitting until virtually the twentieth century. Today when we talk of colour knitting we can include bias-knitted chevrons, intarsia, slip and mosaic work. The machine knitter could add tuck, knitweave, lace with Fair Isle, and double jacquard.

Sue Leighton-White of the Knitting and Crochet

Fig 82
Man wearing a hand-knitted Fair Isle sweater

Guild, who is researching colour knitting, has observed that the length of the yarn floats on many pieces from the late Middle Ages to the eighteenth century, is unacceptable by modern standards. Machine knitters know that the most striking Fair Isle designs are often accompanied by long floats on the reverse side, but the floats on the seventeenth-century jackets in what is known as brocaded knitting, are remarkably long. Richard Rutt thinks that such loose, long floats suggest that the jackets were made on handframes, but there is no evidence to suggest that this kind of knitting was done by framework knitters, prior to the eighteenth century (see Chapter 2). If the charts published by Mrs Gaugain in 1842 were used for colour knitting, then some of the floats would be inordinately long. In the late nineteenth century, there were patterns with floats that spanned nine stitches, as seen on a hand-knit stocking pattern from *Weldon's Practical Needlework*, Vol.II, No.13. On the modern domestic machine, longer floats are more tolerable than in hand knitting, simply because in machine-knit Fair Isle, especially when wool is used, the floats lie closer to the fabric, but we cannot prove that the floats would appear as floppy strands when the knitting was done on a handframe. The other argument against the use of a frame for such knitting is that a number of jackets in collections have the patterns highlighted in reversed stocking stitch. A frame could not do this automatically, and the effect could only have been created by laborious hand tooling.

The nineteenth to twentieth centuries

Colour knitting was less popular with the Victorian drawing-room knitters than was lace, but stranded coloured knitting was used to decorate knitted pin cushions and other accessories. Bands of Fair Isle, intarsia checks and Argylls had made their appearance on hand- and machine-knitted men's stockings by the end of the nineteenth century. Although small amounts of contrasting colours were sometimes used in hand- and machine-knit tops during the nineteenth century, coloured surface patterning did not appear generally on fashionable sweaters and jackets until the Fair Isle boom from the mid-1920s onwards.

Fig 83
Brocaded waistcoats, c. seventeenth century

Colour knitting and the garment shape

In *Needlework for All* (March 1910), it is evident that the editor had quite an interest in historic knitting. She directs her readers to study the beautiful brocaded coats in the Victoria and Albert Museum and her comments throw an interesting light on the level of hand-knitting competence in 1910. Knitters of the sixteenth and seventeenth centuries, she wrote, 'were considerably more ambitious . . . than the generality of knitters'. Time, she observes, must have been 'a less precious commodity than it is today'. She could have mentioned that some of the jackets she so admired were sewn rather badly from near-rectangular pieces of knitting. The mastery lay in the colour and design of the beautiful floral and leaf surface patterns done in silk, and silver and gilt threads. Most of the surface patterns are large even by our standards. Some of the patterns are counterchanged in the second repeat and turned round to face the opposite way. It is no wonder that people have suggested that the garments were knitted on a frame, since this is the kind of pattern-making which machines do rather well. Floral and leaf motifs are currently enjoying a revival as repeat patterns in colour knitting.

No one really knows how the Victoria and Albert Museum's jackets, or waistcoats as they were called, were accomplished. What is significant is that the dropped shoulder line style with little or no armhole shaping presents an uninhibited canvas for the display of large, colourful patterns. Moreover, this garment shape, knitted circular, has been the choice of the hand knitters of Fair Isle and the Shetland Isles from the 1920s until today. To judge from their glossy pattern books, modern hand- and machine-knit designers appear to have tied themselves almost exclusively to a looser version of the dropped shoulder line shape, knitted flat in four pieces. This garment type, knitted sideways as well as conventionally, is very versatile and has had several interpretations. The problem now is how to adapt to the changing fashion for more streamlined styles and subdued jacquards and colour patterns. Designers and knitters ought to be able to move between styles with ease. To stay with one shape exclusively does not do anything for knitting as 'fashion'.

Fig 84
Cover of Fair Isle for All *(1957)*

In the late 1950s, Patons published a booklet called *Fair Isles for All – Stitchcraft No.Sc11*. It deserves a mention here because in many respects it points a way forward for us now. In it, Fair Isle is interpreted very loosely to include large single motifs like the heraldic representation on the cover and lifelike animals and birds, stylized flowers and foliage from embroidery sources as well as the more traditional Fair Isle and Scandinavian patterns. There are clever placements of motifs in bands around the hip, wrist and neck; plain ribbed sleeves and deep ribbed welts contrast with dramatic colour and pattern elsewhere; large motifs are used in bands surrounded by small ones and a colour change. In other words, considerable thought has been given to the use of colour and the placement and arrangement of surface patterns, and they are mainly on the fitted sleeve top.

Fig 85
Chart from Fair Isle for All *showing neckline shaping*

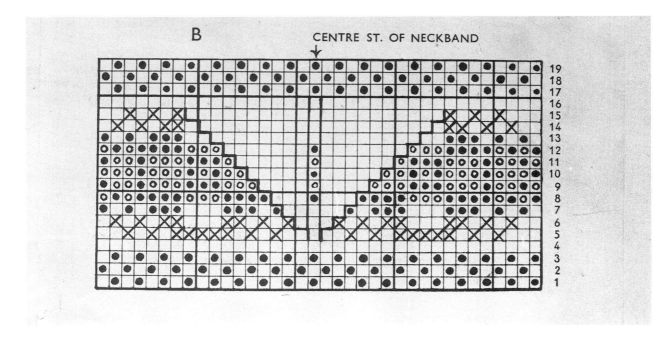

Patons showed considerable enlightenment in this booklet, for charts are used to show the surface pattern and its colour changes. Other spinners of the period continued to give columns of written instructions for colour knitting with not a chart in sight. The charts in *Fair Isle For All* also showed graphically what happened to the pattern at neckline and armholes, and steps in the square gridded graph paper illustrated the shaping.

Stranding, weaving in and twisting

From the time needlecraft publications poured off the presses from the 1830s onward, knitters began to read about knitting styles in various parts of the world. The German way of holding the yarn in the left hand was certainly a talking point from Mrs Gaugain to the editor of *Needlework for All* (1910). The latter recommends that when knitting fancy tops for stockings and ties in club colours, we should knit with one of the threads in the ordinary manner and 'lay the other across the fingers of the left hand and knit it in the German way'. Moreover, when three colours are in use, we should always knit the trimming colour, whichever it is, by the left hand method. In *Woolcraft No.5* (c.1926), we are advised to strengthen the heels of our stockings by either knitweaving an extra thread over and under the stitches, or by knitting slip stitches.

There are no well-defined instructions for weaving in or twisting the yarns behind the

Fig 86
Charts to show woven-in resting colour (hand-knit) and knitweave (machine-knit)

knitting in colour work. I cannot find any clear reference to the techniques we use today until Marjory Tillotson's description in *Modern Needlecraft* (1932), where she gives a written explanation of what Mary Thomas illustrates more graphically by drawings in her *Knitting Book* (1938). Marjory Tillotson also recommends the German way of holding the trimming colour. Though weaving in and/or twisting appear to have been worked alongside intarsia from the 1880s onwards for 'tartan' knitting on stocking tops, it seems that until very recently Fair Isle knitting meant stranding, and certainly this is what it means to a machine knitter today.

When the hand knitter weaves the carrying yarns on the reverse side, so that they lie over the rounded head of the knitted-off stitch and then below it, the resulting appearance is exactly like that of knitweave. Knitweave, as a stitch in its own right, has been known to hand knitters for around 300 years. It is a pattern stitch and not Fair Isle, and the second yarn is not knitted in as stitches. There is a seventeenth-century cap illustrated in *The Art of Knitting*, edited by Eve Harlow, which features the knitweave technique. A form of knitweave was done on the frame in the eighteenth century. Sue Leighton-White has found two patterns for ladies' mittens in Patons' *Knitting and Crochet Book* (1896), one of which gives a clear description of the weaving-in and knitweave technique we use today. In these patterns, the weaving–in of the held yarn is over every second stitch and the mittens were to be worn with the weaving on the outside. Such a use of knitweave is a sensible choice for mitts, since the floats on the

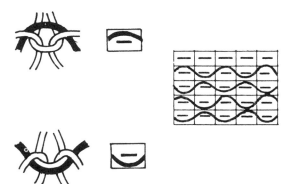

outside cannot be caught by the fingers on the inside. Today, knitweave is done almost exclusively by machine knitters, and is not as popular as it deserves to be with the advocates of colour and texture.

Neither methods nor garments are invented until there is a use for them. In the past, knowledge of knitting techniques was by no means uniform across the community. In most hand-knit patterns today which feature Fair Isle or stocking stitch jacquard, the knitter is advised to weave-in any yarns which threaten to float over more than three stitches. Sometimes the knitter is advised to twist the yarn. Weaving-in and twisting are not the same technique. For one thing, tension gauge is affected by the method we choose, and there is confusion on this point. I cannot think of one book of handknit Fair Isle/jacquard patterns where the problem has been discussed and solutions offered. It would help if writers told us which techniques were used in the sample garments.

When one twists the yarns to take them across the knitting at the back, they lie across the body of the stitch and not above or below it. Moreover, twisted yarns are liable to constrict and distort, resulting in an uneven appearance. When using three or four colours in a row, one cannot help but twist the yarns, as I found when knitting the waistcoat pattern given below. A combination of stranding, weaving and twisting results in a stitch and row ratio that is usually around 1:1, and therefore the use of square gridded graph paper for this type of knitting is correct. Moreover, it is advisable to use the technique in moderation (especially alongside plain stocking stitch), because it produces a thick, dense fabric, particularly in DK yarns, with uneven stitches. Kaffe Fassett's 'Chinese Roses' provide us with an excellent example of this kind of knitting at its best.

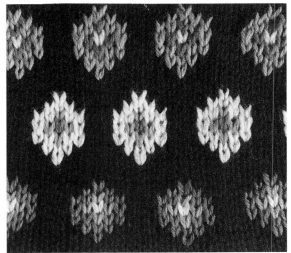

Fig 87
A machine-knitted mini-hexagon slip stitch pattern

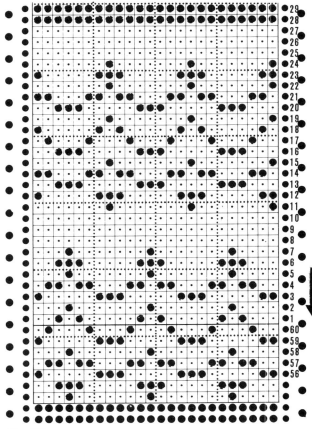

Fig 88
Punchcard for Fig 87

Fig 89a
Mini-hexagon waistcoat

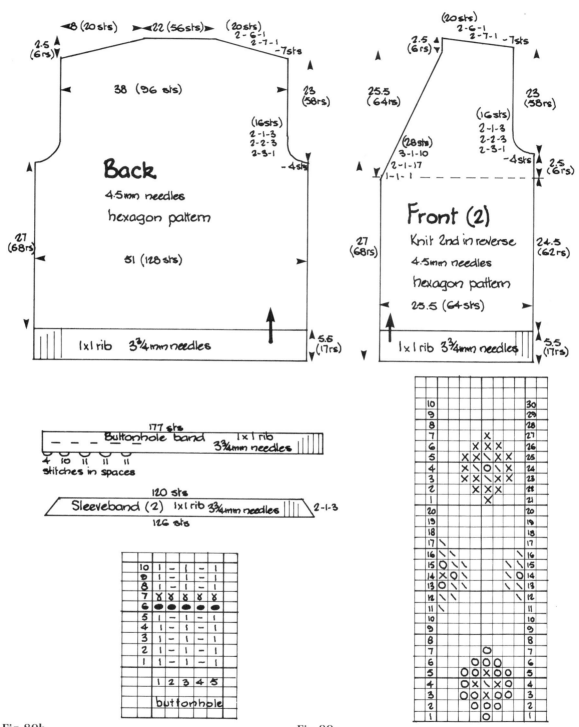

Fig 89b
Mini-hexagon waistcoat – charts

Fig 89c
Mini-hexagon waistcoat – working diagrams

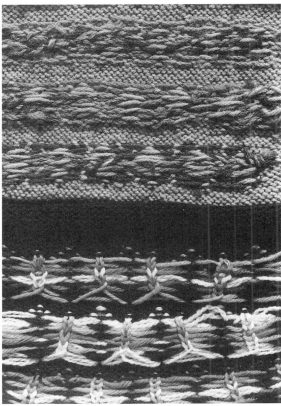

Fig 90
Reverse sides of hexagon pattern showing floats.
Top: *hand-knitted*; bottom: *machine-knitted*

Mini-hexagon Waistcoat

Materials: DK wool: 250g grey, 100g red, 100g pink, 50g each yellow and jade green. 5 buttons.
Size: Bust 102cm (40in). Length 58cm (23in). Width across back 38cm (15in). Depth of V 28cm (11in).
Needles: 3.75mm (US 5) for ribs, 4.5mm (US 7) for pattern.
Tension/gauge: 25sts, 25rs per 10cm (4in).
Directions:

1. Stripes in back/front welts: 4rs grey, 2rs red, 1r grey, 2rs pink, 8rs grey (17rs). Begin main part with 3rs stocking stitch, the first row being a purl row.
2. The pattern has two alternating placements, but three colour sequences.
3. Cast off back neck stitches, but graft shoulders.

4. Stripes on front/armbands: 5rs grey, 1r pink, 1r grey, 1r red, 2rs grey (10rs).
5. Stitches for bands are picked up and knitted outwards. Front bands are knitted in two pieces, 177 sts each, and joined at the back neck.
6. MK. Knit your own version from the pattern in Fig 86.

Note on colour changes: I used two main trimming colours, fuchsia red and pink, in conjunction with yellow and jade green, each worked in rotation. (See diagram.) Each colour sequence had three rows of mini-hexagons: red, pink, yellow; yellow, red, pink; pink, yellow, red, in that order. In the second group of three, green was used instead of yellow. Changing the order of the colours in this way, gives the illusion of more colours than have actually been used. In each mini-hexagon, there are two rows where three colours per row are knitted and one row with four. I decided to leave out a part of one pattern at the edge of the second row and alternate even rows of repeats, to neaten the appearance. The design is seven rows long plus three rows of stocking stitch. Ten rows is an easy unit to check.

When hand knitting the waistcoat, I planned how I could work 3 to 4 colours in a row pattern on the machine without having either to double up the rows and change colours at the same side, or swing the carriage back to collect the yarn on a free move slip row. The technique was quite straight-forward. I punched the holes, row by row, in order of yarn importance. Rows 1 and 2, and 6 and 7, were automatic two-colour Fair Isle anyway, so I left the yarn at the side it landed, collected the next one, and the knitting proceeded reasonably quickly. When I had to break the yarn, I did so without a qualm and left the end to be dealt with later. The machine was the Brother Chunky 260, the yarn DK pure wool knitted on T1.2. The combined settings of Fair Isle, part/slip and stocking stitch produced a tension of 21sts and 25rs per 10cm (4in), a very interesting one, since the gauge for stitches gave me a clue that I was using the slip setting, while 25rs was exactly the same as the one I achieved by hand.

I was particularly impressed by the pattern which stood out boldly like embroidery from its

93

background (dark green). I changed the trimming colours, orange, yellow and white, in order of importance over three rows of patterns as I had done in the hand-knit version and the result was very pleasing. I crocheted up only the top floats as I went along (Fig 90), and that process still left the fabric reasonably supple. There were surprisingly few yarn ends at the edges for the worktool to weave in and out. In all, the experiment was very successful.

The art of motif knitting

To a hand or machine knitter, a motif is a colour pattern with a clearly representational or recognizable image as opposed to a linear geometric form. How this is worked depends on the shape, size and inclination of the motif. Is it symmetrical or asymmetrical? Will repeats benefit from a simple vertical progression? Is the motif better counterchanged and/or turned to face left, then right? Do we place it in the half-drop position in a diamond cameo, like Kaffe Fassett's 'Chinese Roses'? How many plain background rows should be worked between repeats? How are the colours organized; what choice is there for the background and motif? Is the motif suitable for the garment shape? Will the motif need to be re-designed for sideways knitting? Can the motif be used as part of a pictorial display, so that the garment tells a story? Should the motif be used singly, in one row of horizontal repeats, or all over? Does the motif benefit by being placed alongside a different pattern in smaller repeats?

The carnation motif

The carnation has a long association with textile decoration. In England, it dates from at least the sixteenth century when the flower probably first appeared in gardens. Edmund Spenser, in his *Shepheard's Calendar*, mentions the 'coronation', while the unknown lady, whose portrait (*c*.1587) is attributed to John Bettes, has magnificent carnations with turned back lower petals embroidered on her sleeves. A similar carnation motif appeared on Turkish textiles of the same period (see Kaffe Fassett's designs in Kaori O'Connor's *Creative*

Fig 91
Early Victorian pinbox featuring a carnation

Dressing and *Kaffe Fassett at the V and A*). The carnation in the sixteenth century would not have as complicated a flower head as it sports today. Possibly it looked more like a pink. It certainly was easy to stylize, and because of the balanced symmetry of the formalized shape, it was simple to interpret in knitting and embroidery.

From the eighteenth century onwards there are several examples from the great knitted carpets to the little pin cushions of Regency and Victorian times. On Lord Howick's gloves, 1833, illustrated in Richard Rutt's book, there is a row of carnations, square and stilted, but just recognizable. Nearer our own day, there is an attractive carnation in Patons' *Fair Isles for All*, c.1957, which I have expanded and developed into one suitable for a 24-stitch punchcard machine. I have also designed two other versions, one with turned-back lower petals, reminiscent of the sixteenth-century species, and the other I began by sketching from life. I copied one half of my still-life drawing on to a chart and mirror-imaged the other half for easy working, remembering just in time I had hand knitters to cater for as well as those who work by machine (see Fig 95c).

Fig 92
Carnation and support patterns worked as a border

Fig 93
Chart for fig 92

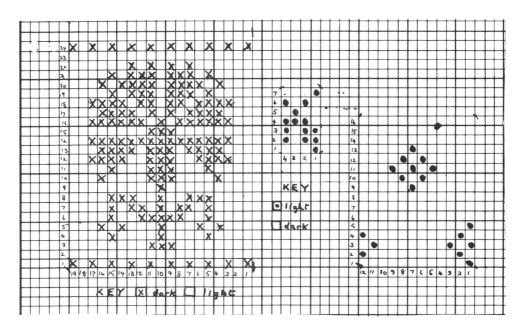

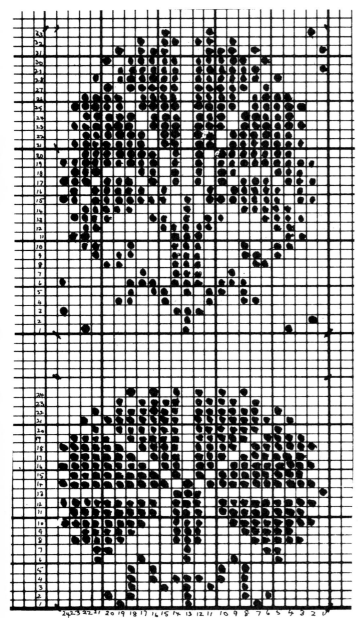

Fig 94
Chart for two carnations (see also fig 96)

Carnation Jacket
Materials: 4-ply wool. 400g pale almond green, 200g clear red, 100g black. 9 buttons.
Size: Bust 112cm (45in). Length 71.5cm (28½in). Sleeve length 50cm (20in).
Machine: Standard punchcard or electronic.

Fig 95a
Carnation jacket

Needles: 2.75mm (US 2) for ribs, 3.25mm (US 3) for main garment.
Tension/gauge: 29sts, 34rs per 10cm.
Directions:
1. Pattern – trimming colours: 8rs black, 22rs red, 6rs background green only. Begin pattern immediately after the welt.
2. Pattern matches at side seams if fronts are centred on the bed.
3. Do second front in reverse to first by using spare main yarn to decrease at neck opposite carriage.

Colour and shape in knitting

In the past, leading hand knitters have sometimes expressed disappointment when Fair Isle/jacquard patterns designed for hand knitting have been machine knitted. To my knowledge, no-one has recognized publicly that we are dealing with two different disciplines and that the designer needs to give considerable thought to the medium in which he/she is working. For example, when I am using mainly two colours on the Fair Isle setting on the

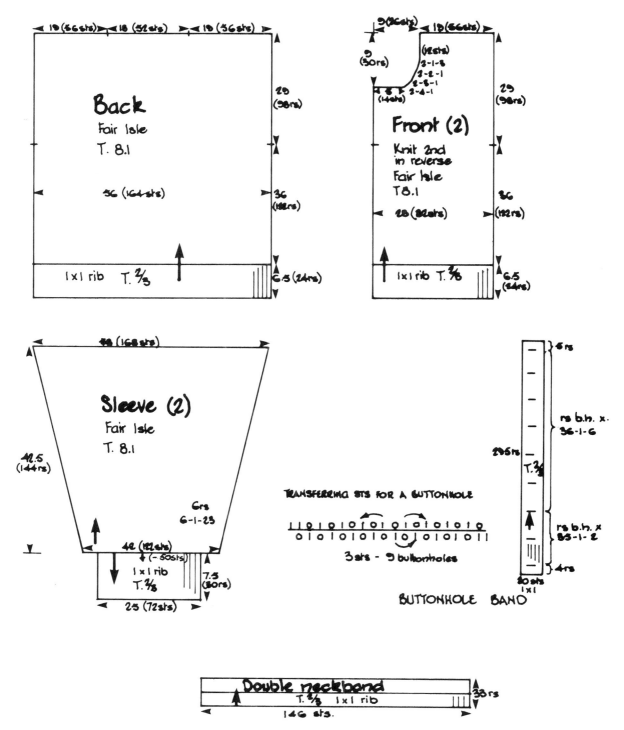

Fig 95b
Carnation jacket – working diagrams

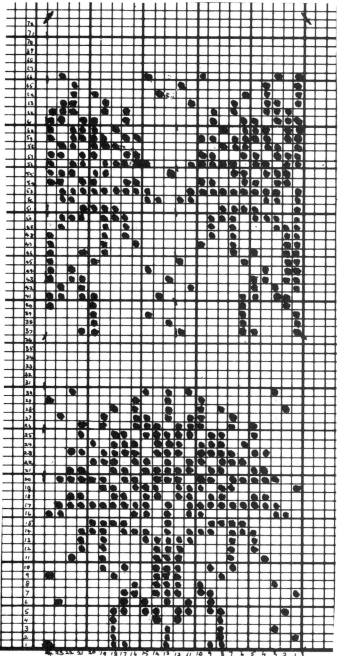

Fig 95c
Carnation jacket – charts

machine, I know that a dynamic shape, which has realism and vigour, stands a good chance of success. Rarely would I hand knit such a motif because of the complexity. A hand knitter, however, can enliven simple and formalized patterns by frequent colour changes within the knitting. Stylized shapes, striped patterns and bald geometric forms are the most difficult of all to machine-knit convincingly in plain yarn on the automatic two-colour setting, unless one resorts to one or more tricks of the trade to achieve an arresting and/or aesthetically pleasing presentation such as that illustrated on page 99. I leave you to consider the argument alongside the three different interpretations of the carnation. If you sample them in each discipline you will see what I mean. Study the poppy also for the effects used (see Fig 6).

Intarsia

Intarsia referred originally to a type of decorative wood inlay developed in Italy in the fifteenth

Fig 96
Three carnations

Fig 97
*A trick of the trade – diagonal negative pattern
dissecting horizontal pattern bands (*Profitable
Machine-Knitting, *Helen Kinder)*

century. In knitting it refers to colour work usually
done in stocking stitch which has no floats because
the yarns are interlinked at the edges. When hand
knitting, it is possible to use the intarsia technique
in conjunction with stranding, twisting and
weaving-in, if the repeatable motif unit is large
enough to be assigned its own palette of yarns. The
knitter can then strand or weave within the unit.
Consider which technique is best for the design.
The pattern instructions may not give all the
options; it is the pattern writer's job to recommend
the methods and techniques used in the sample
garment.

In machine knitting, there are two kinds of
intarsia. One is worked in HP, whereby one colour
is knitted at once over a block of WP needles, while
the rest are in HP. As the groups are re-introduced
from HP to WP, or vice versa, usually every other
row opposite the carriage, then geometric blocks of
colour appear. This type of intarsia is comparatively new, being around 100 years old, and can
only be done on a machine with a holding cam
system. The old handframe had no such system.

The other kind of intarsia is the pictorial and
geometric type, where many colours are laid across
the needles. It originated at least from the eighteenth century and appears to have been used first
by framework knitters on the stocking frame to
cope with a fashion for brocaded waistcoats, as an
alternative to stranding. Some time ago, a
photocopy was sent to me of a drawing of the
invention of John Robertson of Edinburgh, who in
1809, patented an attachment for the stocking
frame to allow the use of up to 11 colours in the
'weaving', *i.e.* knitting, of tartan. I was reminded of

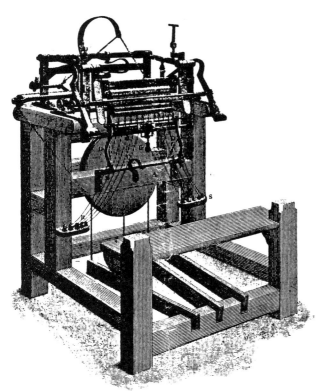

Fig 98
John Robertson's intarsia hand frame, 1809

Fig 99
Tartan checks worked in double jacquard

Fig 100
*A 'charming jumper' featuring intarsia
(Woman's Life, 1934)*

the adage that there is nothing new under the sun, because the device is very similar to the intarsia yarn brake which can be acquired for the domestic machines of today.

Intarsia began to be practised by hand and machine knitters much more widely from the 1880s onwards. Argyll patterns and large checks became popular on sports stockings for men. In a Harrison circular-sock machine pattern of *c.*1880, instructions are given for a cycling stocking with coloured diamonds decorating the top. Three different colours are used and half a diamond is knitted in each of the colours in order across the needles. The needles for the half diamonds not required are 'depressed' – placed in NWP. Each yarn knits each half diamond in turn and the knitter raises needles as required. When the bottom halves are all knitted, the knitter proceeds to the top halves. This form of intarsia looks very similar to that we do today, but it is classed as the NWP variety.

In the first edition of Patons' *Universal Knitting*

Book (1899), there are two patterns for hand-knitted socks, one pair in a simple diamond and the other in Shepherd's tartan. From the instructions, it appears that a mixture of intarsia and weaving/twisting techniques were employed. The knitter is told in the simple diamond pattern that, 'the wool not in use is carried along and knitted in at the back'.

Three yarns are used, a black and white mixture, black and white. The mixture yarn is left in a ball, while the black and the white are worked in short lengths. The mixture wool is knitted in. No long loops appear on the wrong side. The knitter is advised to 'run or knit the ends in neatly', but nowhere is it explained how to knit-in the spare yarn. It is assumed that the knitter will know.

In a *People's Friend* issue of 1905 there is a pattern for stockings in Macgregor tartan which looks just like the Shepherd's tartan of 1899 and the instructions for knitting are the same. This time, though, we are advised to wind short lengths of wool on to pieces of cardboard. We then cut a slit in the card and fasten the wool. These must be the original intarsia bobbins.

On the front cover of the magazine *Woman's Life* (17 March 1934), there is a 'charming jumper'. The geometric intarsia is certainly interesting, but the epaulettes remind one of three long Frankfurter sausages slung over each shoulder. Such is the impact of a fashion of over 50 years ago. The yarns are to be 'twisted' at the edge of the colour blocks. The written instructions are three full columns long and there is not a chart in sight.

Fig 101a
Sweater featuring mohair intarsia butterfly

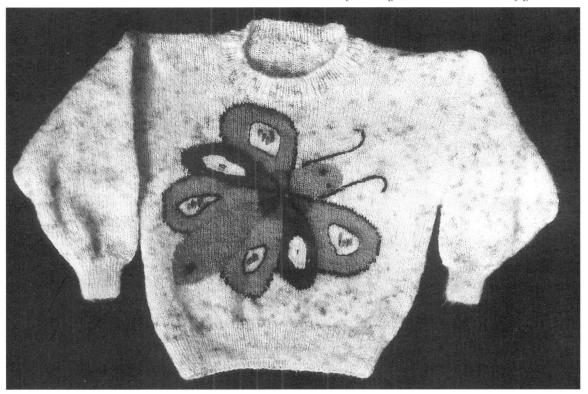

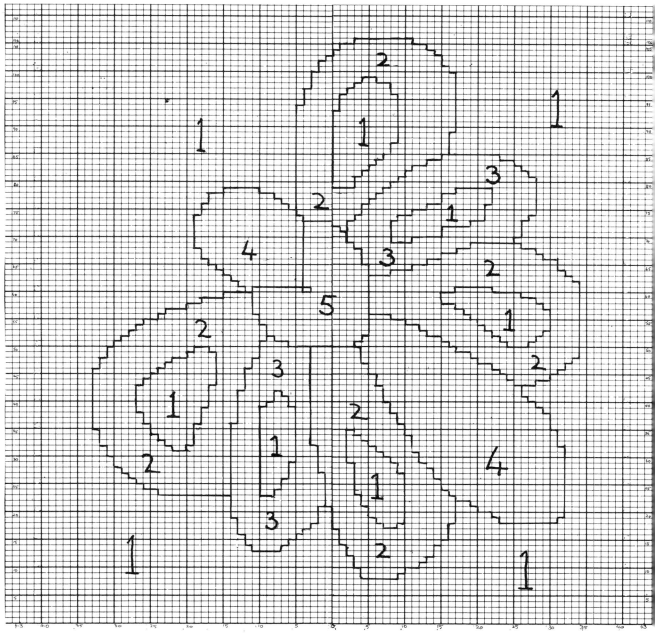

Fig 101b
Intarsia butterfly – chart

Intarsia today

Knitting using motifs has been very popular, right up until the present time. This type of knitting includes large single motifs, such as the butterfly sweater I have designed for both hand and machine knitters, and which I knitted on the Brother 260 machine. Intarsia can be done on any basic chunky with intarsia facilities, and can indeed be produced on a standard machine, but of course the design on the same scale of graph paper will come out smaller in the knitting.

102

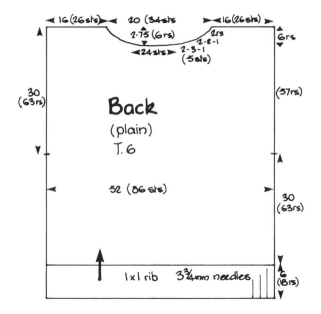

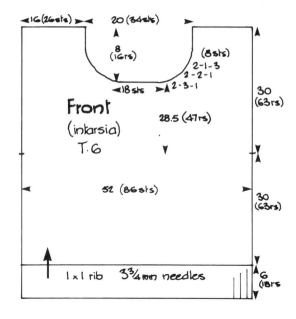

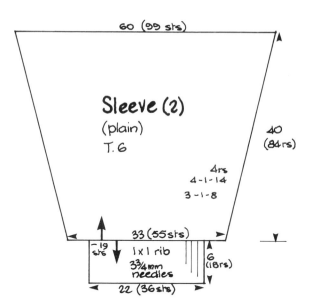

Fig 101c
Intarsia butterfly – working diagrams

Single neckband 1×1 rib T.4

Mohair Butterfly Sweater
Materials: Mohair: 425g spot dyed cream, 300g orange, 50g grey, 25g red, 25g blue, plus small amount of black and yellow for embroidery.
Size: Bust 104cm (41½in). Length 66cm (26½in). Sleeve length 46cm (18½in).
Machine: Chunky with intarsia facility.
Needles: 3.75mm (US 5) for ribs, 4.5mm (US 7) for main garment.
Tension/gauge: 16.5sts, 21rs per 10cm (4in).

Directions:
1. Key: 1 – cream, 2 – orange, 3 – royal blue, 4 – grey, 5 – red. Embroider antennae, markings and spots as shown.
2. Begin pattern on r 9 and finish on r 106, 4rs before front neck shaping.

The popularity of intarsia has encouraged many spinners to provide charts, and knitters who protest that they couldn't possibly knit other stitch patterns by charts, follow the ones for intarsia without complaint. Please note, hand knitters who follow the butterfly pattern should begin on a purl row, or else the pattern will come out in reverse to mine, but will be the same as on the chart. It is a good idea to photocopy and colour the chart. Clip the photocopy to a board or a stiff card and use an elastic band as a row marker. If machine knitters photocopy the chart on to tracing paper, they can follow the reverse image to produce an exact copy of the one on the original chart. On the machine, you can use the chart on the charting device. Select the correct stitch ruler and find the row setting which will allow the depth of one mini-grid to be knocked down at a time. If you use the charting device as an intarsia guide you cannot use it in the normal way. Therefore all breakdowns must be calculated. Finally, don't attempt to darn in loose ends at the end of the knitting. Weave the short ends in and out with a work tool. It is much faster than the time-honoured method and does just as good a job.

In the pattern, I Swiss darned the single stitch detail on completion. There is an alternative on the knitting machine. We call it the one-needle technique. If there is a one-stitch outline to follow vertically, knit this one stitch back to B position by hand with a piece of yarn in the appropriate colour. Lay over the other yarns and link in front of the set-back needle. On the next row, the intarsia cam will bring the needle back to UWP, and the single stitch will be locked behind the crossover. You can repeat the process as often as necessary.

If you plot an original design on a smaller scale of graph paper you will get a proportionately larger knitted image. Graph paper sheets featuring different scales of grids are as valuable to the intarsia as to the motif designer. It means that you need not reject any suitable picture, large or small. Machine knitters who have a charting device, can of course draw the picture straight on to the sheet. They then decide on the colours as they knit, and as the lines of the drawing strike the stitch ruler. If the line goes between colours, decisions must be made. If you make a mistake, Swiss darn over it. For your first attempt choose a simple picture.

Such has been the interest in intarsia, that the facility has been built in to the most recent standard

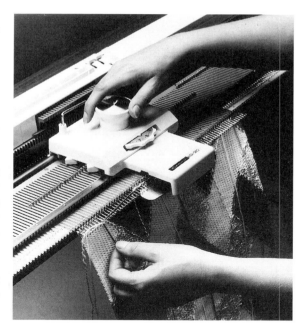

Fig 102
Knitmaster intarsia carriage

models. Whether you are a hand or a machine knitter, it is important to have a little weight on the yarn. Special intarsia bobbins can be bought, or you can make them yourself out of card as per *People's Friend* of 1905. The type of bobbins sold by Brother are particularly good. However, you can wrap small amounts of yarn around a spring clip clothes peg and grip the end in the metal jaws. When I am knitting with short lengths I use intarsia bobbins, or if I haven't any of the latter, spring-clip clothes pegs. When a new yarn is introduced, I lay it over the needles on the machine, grip the yarn end with a clothes peg and let it hang some 30cm (12in) below the needles so that it will not rise up and do battle with the carriage. This is much quicker than tying the end to a clamp and it also means that you can use quite small pieces of yarn. Except where there is a straightforward diagonal progression, and therefore a self-wrap, adjacent yarns must be linked to prevent a hole. On the machine, bring the second yarn from behind to follow on in front of the first yarn. By hand, knit yarn 2 from behind yarn 1. When you knit with yarn 2, the yarn should be linked.

EIGHT

The fitted sleeve shape and garment design

The first major knitted body garments with or without sleeves were no doubt worn beneath top clothes, simply because it wasn't the fashion to wear them on top until nearly the end of the nineteenth century. It is interesting that the first part of the main body garment to appear on top was the sleeve, and separately knitted sleeves, dating back to the sixteenth century, are in the collection of the Museum of London. Patterns for separately knitted sleeves are to be found in Victorian needlecraft manuals. We have already seen that the brocaded waistcoats of the seventeenth and eighteenth centuries were based on the dropped shoulder line shape. All early body garments, whether in one colour or in several, were based on the dropped shoulder line shape. The Charles I vest is no exception. It is also very similar to the gansey-

Fig 103
Ladies' hand-knitted sleeve – 'useful also for charitable purposes' (Mrs Leach, 1886)

Fig 104
*Ladies' fancy cardigan stitch coat with semi-raglan sleeves (*Harrison's Machine-knitting Manual, c.1895–1900)

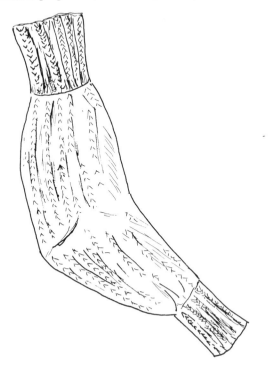

style body garments produced by folk knitters in various parts of the world.

During the nineteenth century, some sleeve-head shaping on babies' and children's wear began to appear in pattern books. In Chapter 2 I referred to a gentleman's cardi-jacket in *Mrs Leach's Fancy Work-Basket* where the sleeve cap was shaped by the short row method but sleeves seem to have been knitted in several other ways too. On a child's jersey in one pattern, the stitches are picked up around the armhole and knitted down, gansey fashion. The sleeve stitches on a baby's matinée jacket are also picked up and knitted down. This pattern is particularly interesting because for the first time we see a semi-fitted sleeve. It must have occurred to the designer that a more closely fitting sleeve shape with less bulk under the arm would provide greater comfort for a small baby than would a miniature fisherman's gansey. A Harrison machine manual, *c.*1890, features adult sweater and jacket patterns with 'raglan' sleeves where the

Fig 105
Baby's matinee jacket. Hand-knitted in 1987 by Doris Harrison from an 1886 pattern

shaping curved to make the diagonal almost like the outline of the fitted sleeve cap but the first specific hand-knit reference to raglans is 1913.

Developments from 1900 to 1940

In Flora Klickman's *Modern Knitting Book* (1916), there are excellent photographs of the pieces of a child's feather-stitch jacket with an armhole cutout which has affinities with Mrs Leach's little matinée coat of 1886. To modern eyes, though, the sleeve and cutout shapings look decidedly odd. Moreover, the shoulder is set at an unbelievably steep angle. Noticeably, and despite the adverts for Baldwin's leaflets featuring ladies sports sweaters and jackets, there are no sweater/jacket patterns for women in Flora Klickman's book. Her work must be regarded as a barometer of 1916 hand knit practice, as she was a leading authority at the time.

In Weldon's *Shilling Guide for Fancy Work* (1914–16), there is an interesting, but isolated, example of a pattern for a ladies' coat, sideways knitted in a fancy garter stitch. The sleeves have a raglan shaping and the shallow armhole cutout is

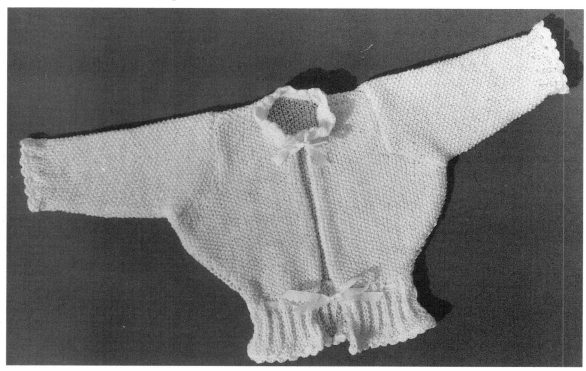

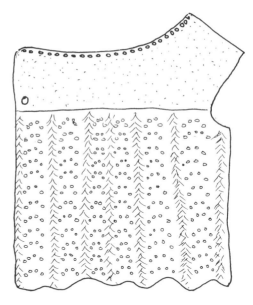

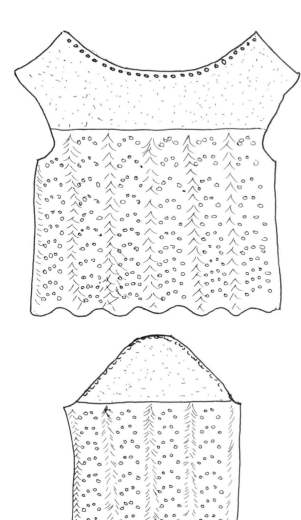

Fig 106
*Pieces of a child's feather stitch jacket
(Flora Klickman, 1916)*

square. Separate leaflets for ladies' tops continued to be published for a number of years, before the styles were considered popular enough to be included in the standard knitting manuals. In the 6th edition of Patons and Baldwins' *Universal Knitting Book* (1923), there are no ladies' sweaters and jackets, but there are patterns in *Woolcraft no 8* (*c.*1929) for ladies 'pull-overs' and cardigans in a simple dropped shoulderline style.

For the most part, until the late 1920s and early 1930s, there was little attempt at shaping the fitted sleeve head in the way we do today. Since the first 'fashion' knitting patterns of the 1920s were based on those from dressmaking sources, the designers – in their progress towards fully-fashioned shaping – had an enormous task on their hands. In addition, they were concerned first and foremost to interpret the currently popular style and that was the fitted sleeve shape.

Around 1932, in women's magazines, little garment diagrams were published annotated with the essential measurements. These showed slight armhole cutaways and curved sleeve heads. A leader in the field was, again, Marjory Tillotson. She explained in her *Complete Knitting Book* (1934), that the diagrams on scaled graph paper (one square grid per inch), 'are sketched so that each sloped line covers a continuous even series of shapings, ie, the shaping commences at the start of the sloped line and continues evenly along to the end of the line.'

Although Marjory Tillotson tells us to distribute any remainders as evenly as we can at the end of the increases and decreases, it is obvious that she is well aware that this practice will not provide perimeter lines which match those of the diagram. So near was she to the discovery of the Magic

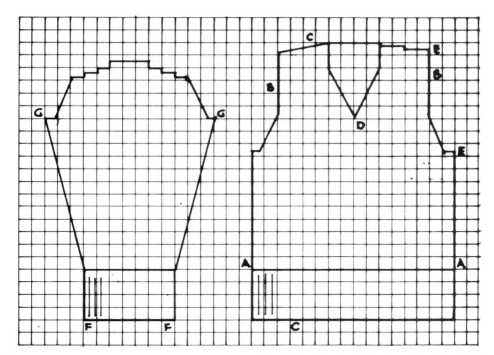

Fig 107
Block for a girl's jersey (Marjory Tillotson, 1934)

Formula and yet so far: 'Occasionally it is an advantage to alter slightly the lines of shaping as first sketched in the diagram in order to obtain a good, continuous even line.' In other words, the knitter alters the diagram to suit the most convenient breakdowns. In 1934 there was no real understanding of how to interpret the line accurately in breakdowns to make the knitting fit the diagram, but at least in the *Complete Knitting Book*, the diagrams are more important than the written text.

Marjory Tillotson's fitted sleeve shape represents an interim stage between the dropped shoulder line and the classic fitted sleeve shape. We recognize her version as semi-fitted and note her attempt at stepping the shaping decreases. On the main body, the armhole cutaway slopes away gradually to around one third in its progress towards the shoulder, cutting away 5cm (2in) at each side. The line EE continues straight to the ball of the shoulder. The sleeve head is particularly interesting. The width from G to G represents the total measurement round the armhole less about 12mm

($\frac{1}{2}$in). The depth of the sleeve head is 6.75cm ($3\frac{1}{2}$in), half of the armhole depth, but 3.75cm ($1\frac{1}{2}$in) deeper than the cutaway. One wonders how this would look. It is always necessary to bear fashion in mind, however, and remember that what looked good to 1934 eyes may not have the same appeal today. Despite this, I cannot help but feel that there was not the clarity of planning that might have been expected. Certainly in *Modern Needlecraft* (1932), Marjory Tillotson presents a shape that is indeed recognizable as a semi-fitted dropped shoulder line. This time the upper arm measurement is exactly that of the armscye (measurement round the arm at the highest point of the socket), and the sleeve head is 5cm (2in) deep, exactly that of the cutaway. This time we feel the sleeve will fit, but why did Marjory Tillotson curve the sleeve head and slope the cutaway? No doubt she planned according to experience and in the matter of the fitted sleeve shape, many hand knitters do just that. Indeed, it is difficult to find one clearly reasoned, step-by-step explanation of why particular measurements are chosen. Nor is it possible to find instructions for how to design and draw a fitted sleeve head in any publication by knitters in the West. If, however, we have not made a study of our knitting manuals published since the 1930s and come to some coherent conclusions, then the Japanese most certainly have. We may have a longer knitting tradition in terms of years, but we have shown little understanding of what we have inherited, and even less ability to interpret it. The neglect and even suppression of our machine knitting heritage is nothing short of scandalous. Even today, amid the growing popularity of machine knitting, many authors use the word 'knitting' in the titles of books, when they are concerned only with hand knitting.

In the 1930s, hand-knitting authorities did not point out clearly that any prospective designer following their principles would require two – unidentical – drafts. One would be used to draw on a body block in suitably scaled, square-gridded graph paper, and the other would be gridded in mini-steps (preferably stitch-proportioned) to show the breakdowns. At that time, no one realised what obstacles this failure to distinguish would put in the way of anyone wanting to design. Neither did anyone attempt to find ways of reducing the effort and the expense. Many modern hand knitters, and some machine knitters, do not know that they can work with one or two mini-sketches for basic shapes and dispense with graph paper altogether. Moreover, an intarsia graph is based on a mini-sketch annotated with breakdowns, which have been previously calculated. Remember that unless the intarsia draft is on stitch-related graph paper, it is not a true representation of the drawing or of the garment's shape.

Mary Thomas's *Knitting Book* (1938), is of major importance in the development of the fitted sleeve shape. Although her instructions are for a no-ease-allowed block pattern, as for dressmaking, Mary Thomas is careful to point out the differences and indeed she gives a valuable and interesting insight into hand-knitting design and practice in the late 1930s: 'The growing tendency is to knit from paper patterns, but these, being constructed for other fabrics, seldom have the simplicity of outline necessary for one of knitted fabric'. No doubt she was well acquainted with Flora Klickman's suggestion of 22 years before regarding the use of paper patterns.

Mary Thomas's block pattern owes a great deal

to dressmaking, for the front is higher than the back and the sleeve cap, somewhat illogically, is symmetrical. She does, however, tell us to draw an S-curve on the sleeve-head and, most interesting of all, the total upper arm measurement is 35cm (14in), which is around 2.5cm (1in) less than the total armscye. Also, the sleeve cap is 12.5cm (5in), two-thirds of the armhole depth of around 18.75cm ($7\frac{1}{2}$in). These measurements were not just arbitrary; they were, after all, based on body measurements.

In contrast, Catherine Franks, in *The Pictorial Guide to Modern Home Knitting* (1939), offers a block pattern which looks remarkably modern. The armhole cutaway, 5cm (2in) deep, is curved, and identical back and front. The sleeve head is curved, too, but not S-shaped. The upper arm width is slightly less than the total armscye and the sleeve cap depth of 10cm (4in) is again two-thirds of the armhole depth of 15cm (6in).

Fig 108a
1940s jumper with bobbles

Developments from 1940 to the present day

It is interesting that two prolific authors, Margaret Murray and Jane Koster, gave instructions in *Knitting for All* (1941) on how to draw a block pattern for a woman's classic sweater. In their version, the armhole cutaway is still 5cm (2in), the sleeve cap slightly deeper at 11.25cm (4½in) and two-thirds of the armhole depth, while the upper arm measurement of 30cm (12in) is again slightly less than the total armscye. The sleeve head has lost its curve and has taken on the appearance of a raglan with straight diagonals and a flat top. This same sleeve shape appeared across the Atlantic in Alice Carroll's *Complete Guide to Modern Knitting and Crocheting* (1942, reprinted by Dover as *Knit and Crochet your own Fashions of the 40s*). The sleeve has, however, lost its diagonal slopes and is curved. Alice Carroll has good advice on how to design puffed sleeves on graph paper. One interesting version requires darts to be shaped and knitted at the top of the sleeve cap. The darts are seamed on completion. Similar patterns are to be found in other publications from the 1940s.

Fig 108b
Diagram for a darted and puffed sleeve, 1940s style

On a number of occasions, when more modern authors have given advice on personalized design, they have tended to follow Mary Thomas as James Norbury did in *Odham's Encyclopaedia of Knitting* (1961). Like Marjory Tillotson 30 years before, James Norbury showed the decreases in steps and offered some advice on designing raglans. However, he set the fashion for rule-of-thumb calculations although no reasoning was offered. Why, for example, is the average sleeve cap depth 13.75cm (5½in)? It would appear that Norbury had faith in the reader's experience and ability to apply the general advice given in the text to the more specific requirements of personalized design.

Some recent advice in the same tradition comes from Debbie Robinson in her book *The Encyclopaedia of Knitting Techniques* (Michael Joseph, 1986). There is a difference in attitude, however. Whereas Norbury gives the impression that ordinary knitters are capable of designing for themselves, Debbie Robinson appears to be in considerable doubt. Her comments are not reassuring, but then she is writing for a post-knit culture generation who have never been offered a clearly thought out programme for learning:

'It takes years of experience (in other words, trial and error) to produce a truly competent designer with the ability to draft patterns . . .

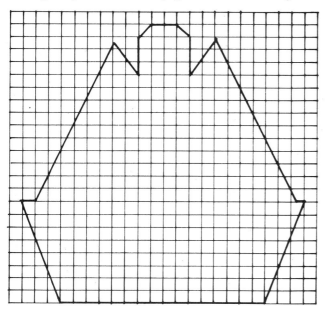

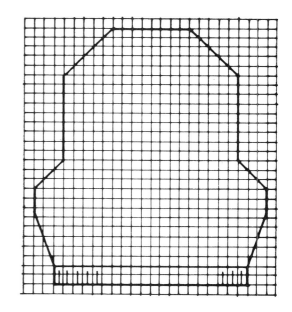

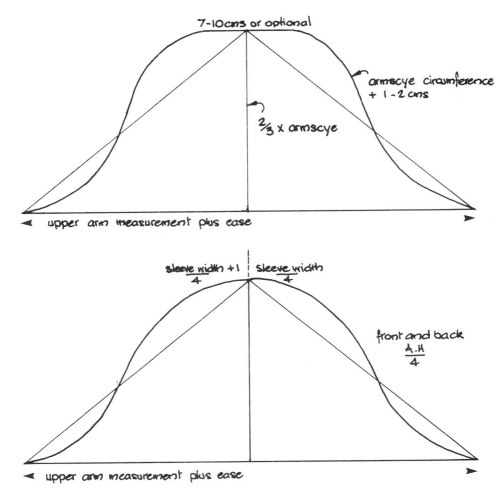

Fig 109
Diagrams for sleeve caps. Top: *symmetrical;*
bottom: *asymmetrical*

Unfortunately, much of the juggling about, rounding up, rounding down, adding odd stitches and rows, here and there, can make the whole process appear incomprehensible. It isn't. Pattern drafting is simply the marriage of logical, arithmetical calculations with the skill and experience to interpret those figures in a flexible way.'

In her *Illustrated Dictionary of Knitting* (1988), Rae Compton gives clear advice on how to take the main measurements for a basic block, but there is no help whatsoever on translating the block to pattern breakdowns. Maggie Whiting is very differ-

ent. In *The Progressive Knitter*, she not only gives a step-by-step approach from design to pattern breakdowns, she offers an easy fitted sleeve shape to follow. It is very interesting that her fitted sleeve cap has raglan diagonals, which take us back to the early machine-knit patterns of the 1890s as well as to the hand-knit patterns of 1916 and the 1930s.

The evolution of the fitted sleeve cap

From my own collection and from the authors whose work I have mentioned, there appear to be two main methods which were developed by British and American authorities in the 1930s and early 1940s. These two methods of designing the fitted sleeve shape have recently been brought sharply into focus by Japanese knit designers:

111

Fig 110
Fitted sleeve dress in knitweave (Lois Franklin)

1. The semi-fitted sleeve shape with a shallow sleeve cap has an upper arm width the same as the armscye.
2. The full-fitted sleeve shape with a two-thirds of the armhole depth sleeve cap and upper arm sleeve shape slightly less than the measurement round the armscye.

The Japanese and the fitted sleeve shape

In *The Knitting Machine Instruction Manual* by Hanai Okamoto (1957), all the patterns are given in the now familiar Japanese diagrammatic form with symbols for the stitches. The fitted sleeves are particularly interesting, because there are quite a variety, which may have to do with the fashion of the time, but is more likely the result of the Japanese approach to knit design. It is a salutary exercise to compare the patterns and the design approach with those of James Norbury, writing only four years later. There is no doubt as to which book has more to offer to the knitter interested in personalized garment design.

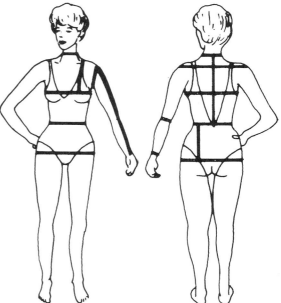

Fig 111
Taking measurements for the basic block

As far as the fitted sleeve is concerned, when close fitting styles are required, the Okamoto manual includes the shallow, elliptical armhole cutout curving outwards to the shoulder ball, so common in the early 1930s. This style is matched of course by a shallow sleeve cap and an upper arm measurement which is a little less than that of the armscye. The curve outwards at the top of the sleeve more than compensates for the loss and will fit with ease into the armhole cutaway. On the other hand, in the Okamoto manual, the less close fitting jackets tend to have sleeve caps of just around two-thirds that of the armhole depth.

The following attractive stitch pattern, which I call festoon lace, is incorporated in a fitted sleeve top and first appeared in the Brother 585 pattern book *c*.1965. The pattern has an 8-stitch repeat, suitable for all lace-making machines. When the punchcard machines came out in the mid-1970s, Brother designers translated many of the 8-stitch patterns for the punchcard machine, but this one is not in any collection. Neither can I find it in any of my hand-knit lace-pattern collections. It seems likely that it was originally from a Japanese source. Festoon lace is what machine knitters call a simple lace, *ie*. no stitch spaces and therefore no leaning strokes between the 'O' and the final decrease. In festoon lace there are two main design units which are very intriguing to study. Please compare the

punchcard with the symbol chart to see how I have translated the pattern. Simple lace patterns look delightful when hand-knitted in mohair and this one is no exception.

For Knitmaster and Toyota 950 lacemakers, the description 'simple' or 'plain' means that you can translate the pattern for the simple or plain lace setting on your machine. I found festoon lace very easy to do. There is very little difference in appearance between the simple and the fashion lace versions. The latter is more textured and is the one hand knitters will choose to do. Punch or mark all the Os made by right to left moves and then on the next row, all the Os made by left to right moves and so on. I used the Knitmaster 560 electronic machine for the sample. Punchcard knitters, punch 3 repeats across the width, and at least 3 repeats vertically (36 rows). If hand knitters attempt this version, they will realize that there are decrease and overs on every row, purl as well as plain.

Fig 112a
Festoon-lace sweater in cotton

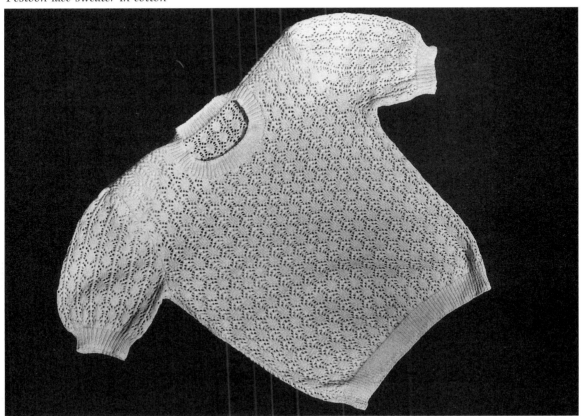

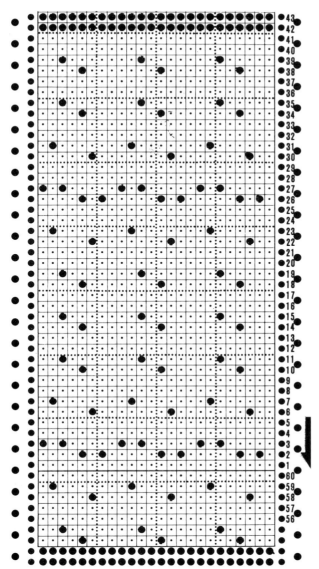

Fig 112b

Festoon-lace sweater – punchcard

Materials: 250g 4-ply cotton. Thread elastic and shoulder pads.

Size: Bust 100cm (40in). Length 60cm (24in). Width across back 40cm (16in). Sleeve length 26.5cm (10½in).

Machine: Standard punchcard or electronic lacemaker.

Needles: 2.75mm (US 2) needles for ribs, 3.25mm (US 3) for pattern.

Tension/gauge: 28sts, 48rs per 10cm (4in) after washing.

Directions:

1. Knitmaster, for fashion lace, copy card as shown, but begin with 2 plain and finish with 2 punched or marked rows.
2. On armhole and sleeve edges, ensure that the first and last two needles on the row do not select and transfer.
3. Wash and press the complete garment before sewing in the pads to fit.

Simple Pattern Drafting for Machine Knitting by T. Seto (Nihon Vogue) is a book widely used by machine knitters. Its alternative title is *Easy Pattern Designing for Knitting*. It was published in 1974, just three years after Nihon Vogue set up its Technological Institute of Knitting in Tokyo to teach personalized design to hand and machine knitters, both professional and amateur. The book (available from knitting machine dealers) is of great value to all knitters seeking to understand how the design of that most difficult of shapes, the fitted sleeve garment, evolved. I have illustrated the relevant points at which measurements are taken for the basic block. From these the Japanese construct a back/front with a square-cutout armhole and the top moving out to the shoulder ball. All drawings are done on graph paper, one square equalling 1cm. The preparations are meticulous and logical, and as the fitted sleeve develops, we see the dotted outline of the block underneath. A total tolerance of 5cm (2in) is allowed. That, of course, will vary with the style.

The way the sleeve cap is constructed is of the greatest interest. First, a horizontal line is drawn representing the upper arm measurement plus ease. A centre perpendicular line is drawn and an isosceles triangle is constructed, each of its equal sides being the measurement of the armscye divided by two. This produces a sleeve cap depth of less than two-thirds of the armhole length. The style is, however, for an asymmetrical sleeve head fitting into an armhole cutout which slopes towards the shoulder and is shorter on the front than on the back. It is no longer as popular with the Japanese as it was in the 1970s.

A fitted sleeve construction which has a two-thirds measurement of the armhole length is

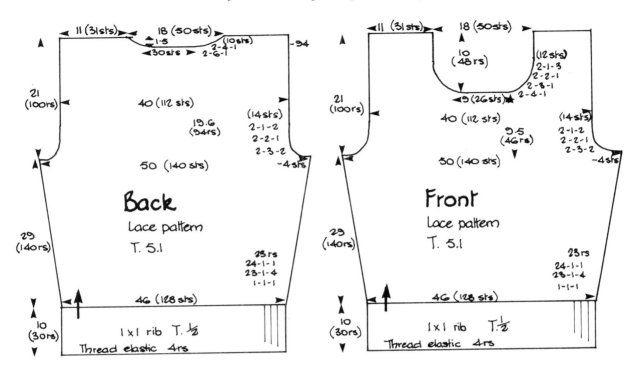

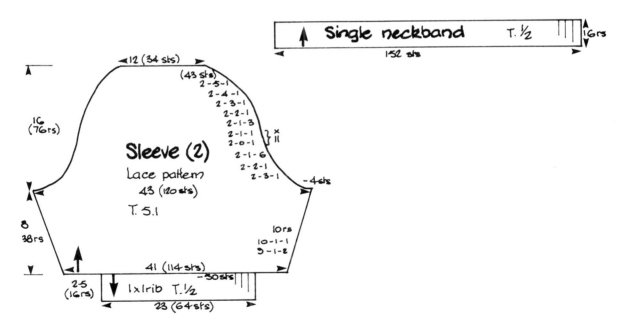

Fig 112c
Festoon-lace sweater – working diagrams

favoured by European designers. Why? One flaw in the earlier Japanese approach was the assumption that the upper arm measurement (plus ease), which is taken well below the shoulder top is the same as the armscye (barely any ease). It is not. As Mary Thomas rightly remarked, it is usually less. The property of two-thirds happens to approximate to the diameter of the armscye circle. It is, of course, not a true circle, but it is near enough. Move your arm up and down, measure for yourself, and you will then understand the argument. In the new, easy fitting sleeve style in vogue at the time of writing the upper arm measurement is often at least that of the armscye matched by a two-thirds depth of sleeve cap, sometimes more. With such a depth, the shape can be symmetrical and there need be no differences in the armhole cutout on the back and the front. When one has patterns to write this style is the only sensible one to choose. The *Passap ABC* illustrates this approach in its garment blocks.

When Knitmaster Knitradar blocks first appeared in the early 1970s, many machine knitters complained that the sleeve shapes did not fit, and

Fig 113
Diagram blocks for the Knitmaster Knit Radar, 1979

we did not see the need for the asymmetrical sleeve head. The whole design was too close to a dress-maker's block. One criticism was that the sleeve cap wrinkled at the top yet was too full a little below. Moreover, knitters quickly realized that there was no need at all to bring out the line of the back/front armhole cutout to meet the shoulder ball. Knitted fabric is so accommodating that it does not require the same kind of treatment as cloth. Indeed, many of the early styles soon slipped over the shoulder and lost their shape. The Japanese obliged and subsequent armhole cutouts were perpendicular and the sleeve head drawn symmetrical. It was not immediately appreciated that to compensate for the loss at the shoulder ball a little more depth had to be added to the sleeve cap.

Some years ago, when I was compiling measurements for 20 sizes of fitted sleeve blocks, I spent many months poring over hundreds of patterns, European and Japanese, as well as studying the guidelines of the Standards Sizings Committee. It was not an easy choice to make, but I have no regrets that I chose the two-thirds of armhole cutout depth for the basic sleeve cap. The armhole cutouts back and front were the same length and rose perpendicular to the shoulder.

When designing for this alternative European sleeve style, it is necessary to draw the sleeve cap

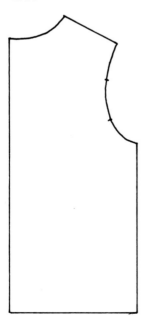 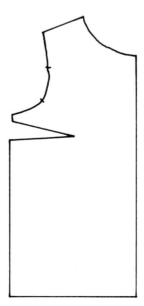 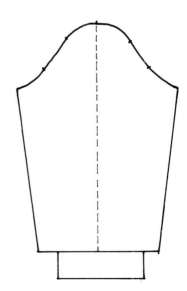

depth across the centre of a line which is usually several centimetres less than the armscye measurement. Compare your armscye (minimal ease) with the top of the arm measurement (plus ease). Next, decide on the measurement at the top edge. The Japanese say it has to be the upper arm measurement plus ease divided by 4, plus 1cm. The total comes to between 7 and 10cm (3 and 4in). In the following Aran cable lace design, I was guided by the width I wanted the centre panel to be at the top. What is important, however, is that the S-curve and the top must together measure the total armscye plus around 2cm ($\frac{3}{4}$in) ease to allow the sleeve to fit into the cutout.

Today the fitted sleeve is fashionable once more and one reason why so much time in this book has been spent on its evolution is because I find that few young knitters understand the principles by which it is designed. Today in Japanese magazines there are many variations, and certainly the fitted sleeve does not seem to be fitting quite as closely as it did 30 years ago.

Fig 114a
Aran lace and popcorn sweater

Aran Lace and Popcorn Sweater

(knitted by Margaret Rhodes)
Materials: 650g Cream Aran Wool.
Size: Bust 102cm (41in). Width across back 37cm (15in). Length 58cm (23in). Sleeve length 56cm (22$\frac{1}{2}$in).
Needles: 3.75mm (US 5) for ribs, 4.5mm (US 7) for pattern.
Tension/gauge: 22sts, 26rs per 10cm (4in).
Directions:
1. Begin pattern with a wrong side row. Therefore, the symbols are read in reverse for this and all odd-numbered rows.
2. Additional symbols ○⋏ = purl 2 tog, ⋏○ = purl one, put back on left needle. Lift second stitch over. Replace on right needle.
3. Shoulder and back neck shaping begin on the same row.

I had great fun deciding what I wanted to put into this garment. The original inspiration came from a hand-tooled pattern in *Brother Hello Knit* (September, 1983), for the chunky machine and ribber. This magazine is in Japanese, published for the Japanese home machine-knitting market. Although I do not read Japanese the symbols and diagrams are very easy to follow. In the original pattern, the Aran lattice was smaller and decorated with large bobbles which I didn't like. Instead of the squashed popcorns, there were tuck stitches over three rows and I suggest that machine knitters wanting to knit this pattern return to the original tuck for the sake of simplicity. Because I enlarged the lattice, I had to lengthen the cable and one out of three ended up with two rows short. Moreover, I re-organized the squashed popcorns on a different repeat base. I originally sampled the conventional popcorns, but felt they were too obtrusive. Finally, I chose one of my own fitted-sleeve garment blocks, slightly amended, in preference to the Brother one. My tension gauge in hand knitting was quite different from the 15sts and 20rs of the original version hand tooled on the chunky machine.

A blow-by-blow account of how a design emerges is often helpful. We may have a starting point, but along the road we make judgements on the suggestions that spring to mind. Often a

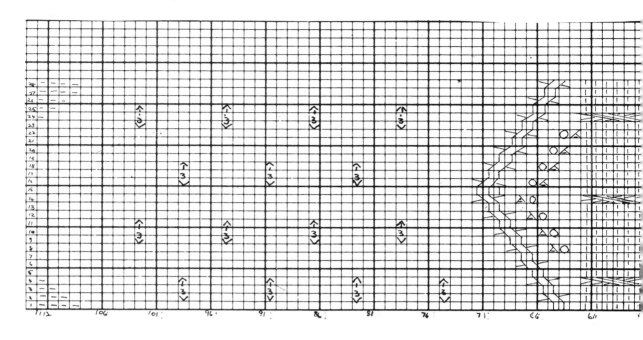

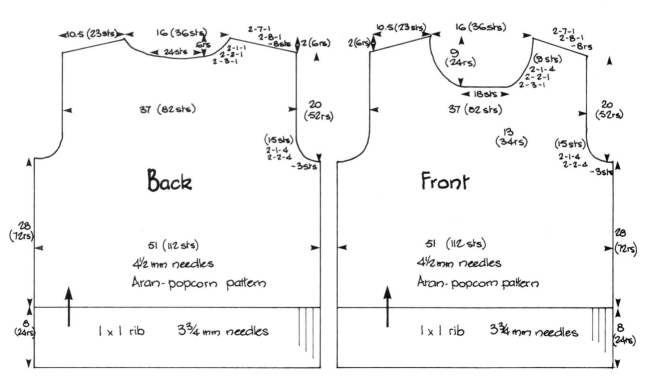

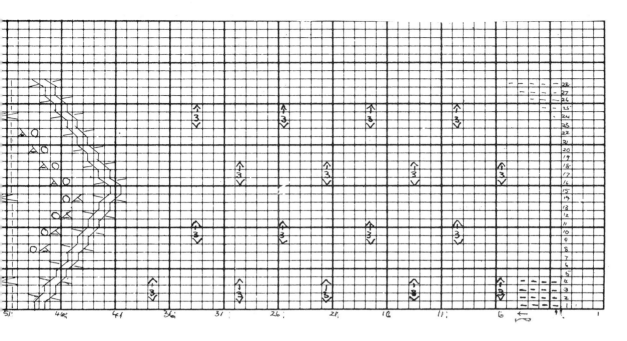

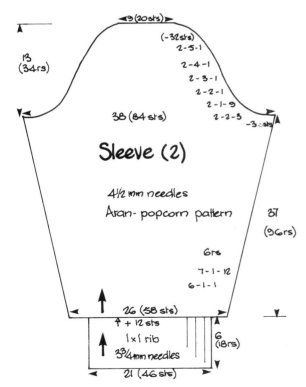

Sleeve (2)

◄9 (20 sts)►

(-32 sts)
2-5-1
2-4-1
2-3-1
2-2-1
2-1-9
2-2-3
-3 sts

13 (34 rs)

38 (84 sts)

4½ mm needles
Aran- popcorn pattern

37 (96 rs)

6 rs
7-1-12
6-1-1

26 (58 sts)
↑ + 12 sts
1 x 1 rib
3¾ mm needles

6 (18 rs)

21 (46 sts)

Double neckband
1 x 1 rib   3¾ mm needles
16 rs
114 sts

Fig 114b *(top)*
Aran lace and popcorn sweater – chart

Fig 114c *(below)*
Aran lace and popcorn sweater – working diagrams

theoretical choice is rejected as soon as it is tried in knitting.

When following the charts on the machine, study them very carefully and decide whether or not you should mark them in reverse to act as a reminder. Normally, stitches for cables are crossed on the main bed, but whether they are crossed there or on the ribber, the stitches placed on top will come underneath on the knit-side. In a simple cable it doesn't matter which way the twist goes, but in a double one it does. In the same way, the Aran lattice has two stitches on top and one underneath

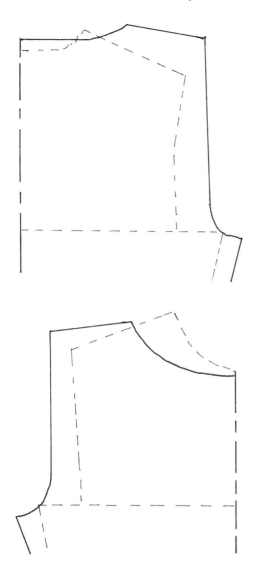

Fig 115
*A Japanese pattern block showing stages in the
development towards a fitted sleeve design*

and therefore on the machine the two stitches will
go first on the needles followed by the one on top. In
this pattern the cables and the lattice are worked on
the ribber and practice is required to get the action
right.

Hand-tooling Arans on knitting machines en-
joyed great popularity in the 1960s, and in New
Zealand there is still a strong tradition for hand
tooling a whole garment. This kind of work does

not accord with today's impatient society but it is
worth doing on a chunky machine as the work
grows more quickly than on a standard machine.

It is easy enough for a machine knitter to draw out
the shapes for the charting device and then just
follow its guidelines, but how does a knitter cope
who hasn't got one? In *Knitting Fashion* (BBC,
1976), Pam Dawson tells hand knitters that if a
design is complicated then it may be better to draft
it out on graph paper. Machine knitters would say
that with knowledge of the Magic Formula it is only
necessary to draft and step out curved sections like
sleeve heads and necklines. Otherwise the whole
design process becomes a laborious and expensive
exercise. Pam Dawson makes an interesting re-
mark which throws light on the practice of British
designers: 'Most professional knitting designers
prefer graph paper where each square represents
one stitch and each row of squares shows a row of
knitting.' She also points out that the mini-gridded
draft makes checking a written pattern easier.
Certainly before the age of the household calculator and of the Magic Formula that would be the
case.

Today, many knitting authorities are agreed
that the grid should be decided by the stitch and
row ratio and that stitch-related graph paper
should be used when necessary. Otherwise, the
sleeve cap shape will appear distorted. In many
cases the grid will be rectangular and not square.
When one has gridded a few fitted sleeve caps in the
conventional way, the realization dawns that there
is a pattern to the breakdowns and the whole
process can then be speeded up.

When I was writing patterns in six sizes, I
worked out many a sleeve head in the following
way. One can only usually manage to knit one
sample garment, after all, and it would be too slow
and expensive to grid out dozens of sleeve heads on
proportional graph paper.

Take a piece of A4 graph paper, five squares per
centimetre. Draw a perpendicular line with a
pencil. Mark off 44 rows on the vertical grid,
1 × 2mm square per row. Write 14 sts against row
44. In approximately the first quarter of the depth,
starting from row 1, and using pencil tally strokes,
write in the decreases as on the underarm of back.

Sometimes, in order to keep the sleeve width correct, it is necessary to decrease fewer stitches. This will depend on the style and/or the stitch and row gauge.

For the centre half of the total depth, allocate 1 stitch. For the last quarter, allocate proportionately more towards the top, say 2, 3, 4, 5, etc. Now count. If you haven't a total of 76 stitches to decrease on the curve, adjust the figures until you have, bearing in mind the proportions above.

Incidentally, I usually managed to work out 6 sizes on one sheet of A4 graph paper.

A geometric approach

Draw the sleeve head and quarter it. Draw short vertical and diagonal lines to make four right-angled triangles. With the aid of the Magic Formula (see page 53), work out the rate of decreases along the curve and arrange the breakdowns into a

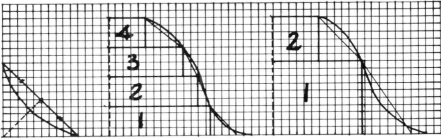

Fig 116c *(above)*
Drawing a curve and stepping a sleeve head

Fig 117c *(below)*
Japanese tools for a knitwear design. Note the special blocking pins

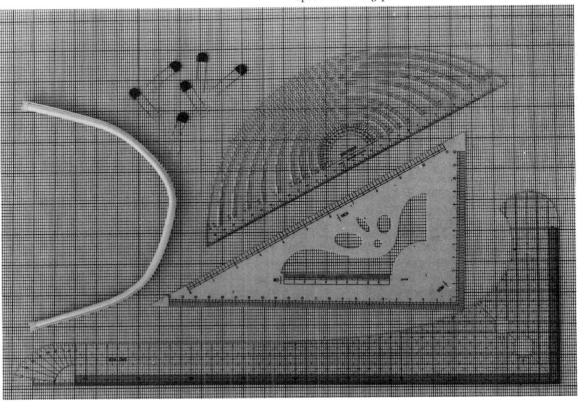

workable order. The sleeve head may appear angular, but the corners are rounded off when knitting. In fact you may well succeed with a sleeve head that has only two triangles from which to make your calculations.

Tools for design

If the garment has a surface pattern like intarsia, you will need to mark out the whole garment shape on stitch-related graph paper, unless of course you are using a charting device. To do this, you will need a set square, a long, straight ruler, a curved rule, pencils and rubber. Most knitting-machine dealers sell some of the tools which the Japanese use in knit design. I find the long, L-shaped triangular rule made by Brother particularly useful as it is about sweater length. Because of this I often use plain paper for the basic block and not expensive graph paper. The Brother triangular rule has square cms marked on its transparent surface, and this makes it very easy to use on paper that is not gridded when drawing and checking lines that should be parallel and at right-angles. Cutout curves on the Japanese rulers are also helpful when drawing armholes, necklines and sleeve heads. The smaller Knitmaster triangular rule is marked in half scale as well as full scale. The flexi-curve is invaluable for measuring sleeve curves, as it is marked with centimetres though I find I can dot the curves fairly accurately with pencil. If I make mistakes, such a dot is easy to rub out and mark elsewhere. A piece of thread is a reasonably accurate way to measure curves and the curved semi-circular rule is designed for drawing a selection of curves in different sizes.

How to begin to draw your block

I have a golden rule which works well: I draw the longest horizontal bottom line and dissect it with the longest perpendicular. The rest of the lines – parallel or at acute or right angles – fall into place alongside these two. Curves are often best drawn below the hypotenuse of a right-angled triangle, as Japanese practice.

Variations on the fitted sleeve shape

I have already discussed the move from the semi-fitted to the fitted sleeve, but once the armhole drops below the underarm many of the principles mentioned do not apply. This is because they belong more properly to the dropped shoulderline shape, where the top straight edge of the sleeve fits exactly against the sleeve depth on the main block, or into the armhole cutout in the basic semi-fitted version. There are several variations on this theme. NB: The 2/3rds depth on a classic fitted sleeve cap usually provides the armscye measurement around the top edge, plus 1 to 2cm for tolerance, to allow the sleevehead to fit into the armhole cutout with ease.

In *The Sweater Book*, edited by Amy Carroll, Zoe Hunt reveals the secret of the spectacular puff at the top of the sleeves on her beautiful Harlequin sweater. One simply reduces the stitches by half by k2 tog across the whole row. Expert hand and machine knitters have many such tips in their repertoire, but each one usually relates to a specific garment and cannot therefore be taught as a general rule. Rule-of-thumb methods do not accord with the precision methods of the Japanese, who mark sections of the back/front armhole cutouts with waste yarn, and align them to the appropriately marked sections of the sleeve. I believe that a mixture of such experience and a more formal approach to knit design should be conveyed to knitters. It is the latter that has been missing in the West up until now.

There are quite a few books aimed at the dressmaker who wants to draft her or his own blocks and design patterns. The Japanese knitting schools teach dressmaking principles with significant differences. On a full gathered sleeve, for instance, the amount of fullness in knitted fabric must be greater than that in woven fabric for dressmaking. Knitting is softer, more pliant and a discreet fold here or a mini-pleat there soon disappears without a trace. Exaggeration is called for. There are various methods that can be employed. Indeed, it is interesting playing around with chopped-up pieces of a paper sleeve pattern just to see what is possible. When you have arranged the pattern pieces to your liking, spread

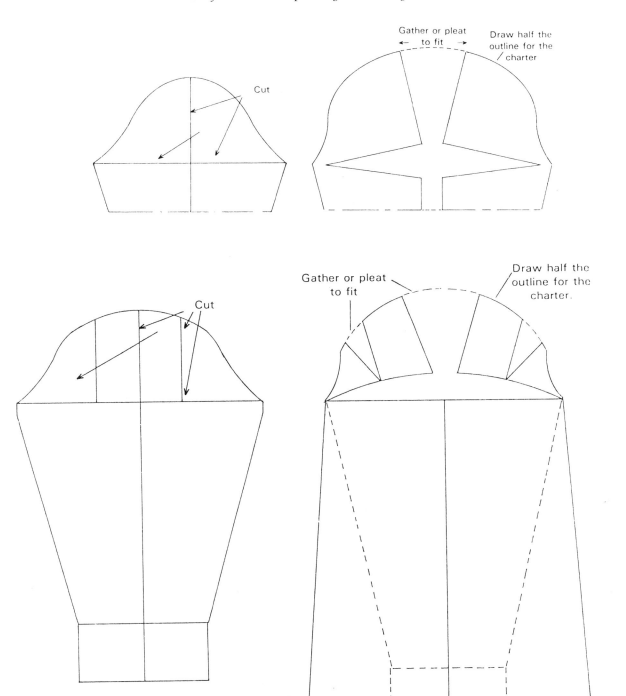

Fig 118
Modifying the basic sleeve cap. Top: *the short-puffed sleeved;* bottom: *gathered full sleeve*

them out on paper and draw around the new shape. It is from the outline measurements of the new shape that your pattern calculations are made. Machine knitters, of course, merely draw the half shape on the charting device sheet.

A quickly drawn, gathered sleevehead

Take a basic fitted-sleeve block and re-draw the top curve of the cap at least 4–5cms (1¾–2in) above the original line. The extra fabric can be distributed on each side of the shoulderline and will provide a slight gathered fullness.

Shoulder pads and the gathered/puffed sleeve head

When shoulder pads are used, the armhole cutout is deeper and the sleeve is therefore larger than the norm because room must be provided for the pad to fit. The measurement at the widest part must be that of the enlarged armscye plus extra for the gather or puff. The sleeve top is then about double the width of the conventional one.

From dropped shoulder line to fitted sleeve

As we have seen, the dropped shoulder line provides a marvellous canvas for bold surface patterns and no doubt will continue to be a popular choice. The fitted sleeve shape on the other hand, usually looks best with less obtrusive surface designs. Features like necklines, stitch textures, suitable collars, bands/edgings, as well as the proportions provided by varying depths of welts, must all be considered for the success of the fitted-sleeve shape. Certainly, collars and necklines assume an importance they do not have in a basic shape. Perhaps the fitted sleeve is more difficult to design and knit than the dropped shoulder line top. It challenges the designer to seek a harmony between surface pattern, colour and structure, and provides an interest and excitement which hasn't been experienced for more than a decade in the field of pattern design. Moreover, no other garment shape highlights the need for a diagrammatic format to show sleeves and armhole shaping clearly, and in my view the Japanese format is really the only one to adopt in the circumstances.

NINE

Circular yokes
and variations on a theme

In the late 1930s, the stone-cutting industry of Bohuslan, a region of southern Sweden, collapsed, and the people fell on hard times. In 1939, Emma Jacobsson, the wife of the governor, who was herself a talented textile designer, organized the Bohus knitting co-operative. Although Sweden has a long tradition of knitting, the Bohus group decided from the onset to strike along new, exciting paths. According to Sheila Macgregor, in *The Complete Book of Traditional Scandinavian Knitting*, (Batsford 1984), one of its most talented members,

Fig 119
Sketch impression of a ladies' jumper with sideways knitted yoke (Woman's Weekly, *1935*)

Ann-Lisa Mannheimer Lunn, produced their first round-yoke sweater in 1949. The distinctive trait of the Bohus yoked sweater was provided by the beautiful, subtle colour-ways used in two-colour Fair Isle and slip stitch over tiny, merging geometric shapes. As time went on, the Bohus knitters included small areas of reversed-stocking stitch in colour to give additional textural interest. The Bohus co-operative disbanded suddenly with the death of its founder in 1967 and also with the return of prosperity to the region. Prosperity and knitting for money never did go well together.

In her book, *Knitting in the Old Way*, the American hand-knitting authority, Patricia Gibson Roberts, gives as around 1940 when the

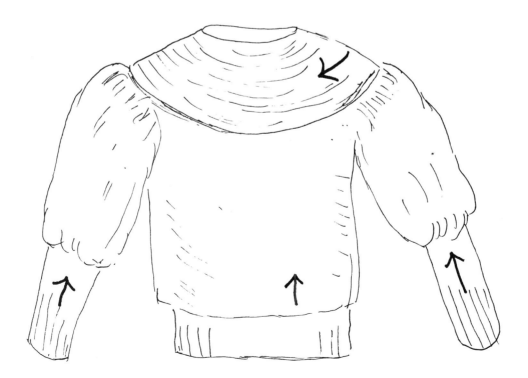

Fig 120
Sketch impression of child's feather stitch yoked sweater (Knitting Illustrated, *1948*)

circular yoked sweater was thought to have been invented by the Bohus knitters. Sheila Macgregor, however, does not specifically say that the Bohus knitters invented the shape and she is right to be cautious. In British pattern literature of the 1930s, there are a number of designs featuring circular yoke styles in a variety of stitch patterns but none has the distinctive, deep, rounded shape and the

colour-ways of the Bohus yoke. It is significant, too, that leading British writers and designers from the 1930s onwards never give specific advice on how to design circular yokes. In *Practical Knitting Illustrated* (1941), by Margaret Murray and Jane Koster, the suggestion is offered to knitters that they might alter a child's high neck jersey to include a 'wide, striped, sunray yoke', yet no advice is forthcoming on how to do it.

As far as the Bohus yokes were concerned, they were unique and subsequently the vogue for circular, coloured yoked sweaters spread out from Sweden into the rest of Scandinavia, to Iceland and to the Shetland Isles. In each of the countries the yoke assumed special characteristics. In Iceland, for example, soft, bulky sweaters, with huge, rounded yokes in geometric icicle designs, knitted in the natural colours of Lopi, soon became a national symbol. In the Shetland Isles, the yokes were smaller and neater and knitted with all the colours and pattern subtlety of the Shetland Island knitters using their finer, softer yarns.

In spite of all the romance surrounding their origin, circular-yoked sweaters are the least worn of all the sweater shapes in Britain. Some designers

Fig 121
Hand-knitted Shetland yoked sweater (Ambery Longbottom)

say that yokes are rarely in 'fashion', and even when they are they are not popular. In the history of costume, however, the circular yoke design had a place in the dress of Tutankhamun, of Henrietta Maria, Queen of Charles I, and of the early Victorians. The yokes (in knitting) which are seen most often today are those from Shetland, where the yoke itself is likely to be hand knitted and then attached to a machine-knitted stocking-stitch body. While many people enjoy wearing yoked sweaters, others complain that the style is not comfortable, that the sweater can ride up and wrinkle on the collar bone, and that the neckline can pull into a boatshaped slit, high at the front and open at the sides. I understood these criticisms better when I went to Shetland and examined some yoked sweaters for myself. There is no shaping on the main body of the Shetland sweater to curve around the bottom of the yoke and the back and

Fig 122
Cover of Patons' Knitting from the Islands

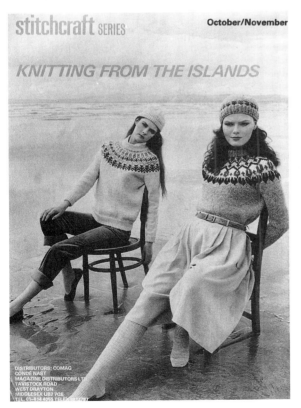

front are knitted the same. Sometimes a little extra of the front yoke is pushed into the double neckband to drop the neck a little. The Fair Isle knitting of the yoke itself is exquisite, often incorporating varieties of the tree and star patterns. The shaping reductions are done in vertical spaces between horizontal pattern repeats. This kind of design knowledge is carried in the head and is not easy to communicate from pattern writer to reader. Certainly it would be difficult for machine knitters to achieve shapings between patterns and so alter the repeat base. It is easier, instead, to teach everyone to begin by shaping on the horizontal plain rows between rows of patterns.

Even with such objections, it is difficult to understand why the yoked sweater is noticeable by its absence in virtually all British hand-knit pattern literature from both spinners and individual designers. A possible exception among the spinners is Patons, the most traditional of all British spinners and the one most mindful of its history. There are several yoked patterns in *Knitting from the Islands* (Stitchcraft series, published in the early 1980s). However, the yoke decreasings which occur within the patterns would be difficult for a machine knitter to do, working within the fixed system of a modern machine. Another of Patons' books, though, *Fair Isle Look*, does include yoke shaping which would be feasible for the machine knitter worked as it is between pattern bands. The publication date of this book is 1975, and it is interesting that Knitmaster's *Modern Knitting* featured several similar yoked designs in the early to mid-1970s. Some of these yoked patterns were sideways knitted too.

The current situation in machine knitting is a little better than in hand knitting. From time to time, magazines feature a yoked sweater. For example, there is an attractive yoke set in a sideways knitted dolman sweater with a co-ordinated flared skirt in *Machine Knitting News* (August, 1987). Knitweave, and not Fair Isle, is the stitch feature used. Individual designers such as Iris Bishop and Marion Nelson, and the Americans Joyce Schneider and Sara Brooks, have published yoked patterns for machine knitters, while in *Easy Fair Isle for the Brother Ribber* (1988), Mary Weaver includes an interesting yoke based on the dropped shoulder line which is different from the one I give in this book. Beautiful yoked sweaters appear regularly in the German Burda handknit magazines, both English and German language versions, while American hand knitters have become the specialists in the English-speaking world. The Japanese, however, are the one national group who have explored the yoked sweater in all its variety and complexity, in a multitude of stitch patterns and with a graphical precision and clarity communicable to all. I have not only learned the technique of yoke design from Japanese pattern diagrams merely for myself, I have understood it sufficiently to pass on to others. What I have learned I have found nowhere else.

Yoked sweaters: the American handknit contribution

In *Knitting without Tears* (1971, Scribner), Elizabeth Zimmerman describes her highly original approach to circular yoked sweaters. She was one of the first knitters to discover that a back yoke, higher than the front, made for a more comfortable garment, and she is right. A yoked sweater I machine knitted from an early 1970s pattern was the same back and front and it was not really comfortable to wear. Elizabeth Zimmerman's sweater is virtually seamless, and there is nothing new in that for hand knitters. What is new is the percentage method she worked out for the design of the yoke. She tells the reader to follow the percentages she has worked out, but doesn't give the reasons for her choice.

Though there is a fuller explanation in *Knitting Workshop* (1981), there are few drawings in Elizabeth Zimmerman's book to illustrate the percentage system clearly. She relies almost entirely on the power of her writing to persuade us to pick up our needles and try, and indeed she succeeds. She also caters for those women who are 'afraid' of maths, and it is rather sad that she still feels the necessity to do this.

There are, however, some bold, explanatory drawings in *Knitting in the Old Way* by Priscilla Gibson Roberts, to show what percentage of the total body measurement one takes at various stages of the yoke. The author also explains to hand knitters that when they want to decrease stitches

between a row of patterns horizontally and so alter the repeat base, they must think of the whole yoke as cone-shaped and distribute the stitches equally throughout. In this type of calculation there is always the danger that the sweater is knitted to fit the pattern and not the person.

Elizabeth Zimmerman, Priscilla Gibson Roberts and fellow American, Jacqueline Fee, whose *Sweater Workshop* is also a classic, are all folk knitters, updating and imbuing with new life the old European tradition of knitting in the round with wool. They exemplify the way in which a nostalgic love of the folk knitting of the Old World can blossom and bear fruit in the New. Their interests and attitudes could not be more different from those of the writers of the British designer Knitwear Revolution.

The Japanese approach to yokes

The Japanese approach is geometric and mathematical. If you are a woman and are conditioned to feel 'afraid', just consider the alternatives. You either explore new, exciting ways, and have more design options than you can possibly cope with, or you stay well within the limits of your capabilities and do not use your initiative or tax your intelligence. The choice is yours. To work with the Japanese system, you will require a calculator, pencil, paper, rulers, a drawing pin and a piece of fine string to serve as a pair of compasses. Most important, you will require a basic garment block annotated with measurements.

Circular yokes can be designed and knitted on any garment shape, dropped shoulder line, fitted sleeve or raglan. They can be incorporated in dolmans and full-blown batwings and can even form a cap-sleeved top on a summer blouse. The latter style was popular in the 1930s, and is a favourite with today's Japanese designers. Yokes can vary in size from a wide collar to a full-blown circular yoke, cutting well into the sleeves. When designed on the fitted sleeve shape, however, they do not usually involve the sleeve.

You will need to draw out the block on paper, incorporating the yoke as you do so. The yoke has to be dissected by lines according to the patterns you have chosen. The lines are then translated into stitches and rows. You use the Magic Formula to get equal distribution of the stitches to be decreased, or increased if you choose to knit the yoke from the neck down. You can knit yokes sideways, as well as in the conventional way and they can be knitted in any suitable stitch. Fair Isle is the most common, but yokes can be worked in lace, cables, ribs, knitweave and textured patterns of all kinds. Simple stripes and shadow pleating from thick and thin yarns also make very effective yokes.

Note on sideways knitted yokes

If you knit the yoke sideways, you must first decide how many segment divisions you require – these will be the flares, plus small unshaped sections which can feature patterns. The latter will converge on the neckline. Take away the measurement of the neck circumference from that of the yoke, and you have the measurement for the flares.

For the purpose of the Magic Formula breakdowns, each flare is an isosceles triangle made up of two right-angled triangles. The Magic Formula breakdowns for short-rowing one of the right-angled triangles are reversed for the second.

The chunky machine and the circular yoke

You will need to use a chunky yarn to give no more than 16sts per 10cm (4in) on Fair Isle, or else you will not have sufficient needles with which to knit a full yoke in two pieces. You can always re-draw the yoke so that it is shallower. I have found that three ends of 4-ply oiled Shetland give an Icelandic Lopi appearance. The yarn is soft and the garment not

Fig 123
Top *with ribbed yoke* (A Machine-knitter's Book of the Ribber, Vol I, *Kinder*)

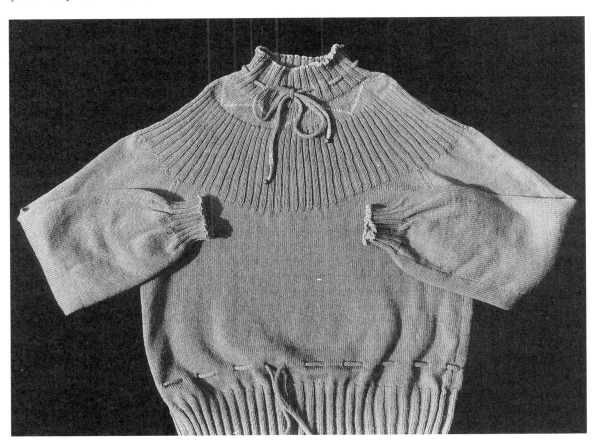

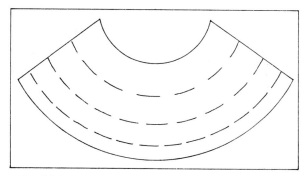

Fig 124
Yoke showing three lines for decreases

too heavy. You will soon evolve your own system for stitch reductions. When I knitted the following pattern, I divided the 66sts I required to lose between the three repeats of the pattern and the result was very successful. Note that 4–5cm (1¾–2in) are reserved on the back front and sleeve to form a gusset underarm. It is best to draw out the yoke to see why this provision is necessary. This style is by far the easiest to design and knit. The Japanese have several versions based on the same idea and it is worth studying their patterns.

Chunky circular-yoked sweater

Materials: 2/8s oiled Shetland on cone, used 3 ends throughout: 350g denim, 100g each of pale blue and white, 75g each of lilac, pale grey, lavender and dark purple.
Size: Bust 100cm (40in). Length 64cm (25½ in). Sleeve length 43.5 cm (17½in).
Machine: Brother 260 chunky punchcard.
Needles: 6mm (US 10) needles for stocking stitch, 6.5mm (US 10.5) for Fair Isle and 4.5mm (US 7) for ribs.
Tension/gauge: Stocking stitch, 15sts and 21rs per 10cm (4in); Fair Isle, 16sts, 20.5rs per 10cm (4in).
Directions:

1. Key: A (main) denim, B pale blue, C white, D lilac, E pale grey, F dark purple, G lavender.
2. On punchcard begin to mark 7rs up. For pattern 1 turn punchcard upside down.
3. Finish back with 2 lots, front with 3 lots and sleeve with 4 lots of WY.
4. Yoke – MK: Begin pieces with WY. Mark centre stitch. HK: Pick up centre sts on back, two half

Fig 125a
Chunky yoked sweater

sleeves, then front and two half sleeves. ALL: Reduce sts on first row of stocking stitch after pattern. MK: Scrap off in WY and replace.
5. All knitters. Graft 7 sts at each side of front to 7 sts on each sleeve. Graft each raglan slope on back to 7 sts on each sleeve.
6. Mattress stitch or figure-of-eight graft yoke pieces on one shoulder. Apply neckband before closing other shoulder. MK: Graft yoke to main body.

Designing the basic raglan shape

The raglan is the most recently developed of the three main top garment shapes (dropped shoulder line and fitted sleeve being the other two), and it has been a popular choice for yoked sweaters. In the second volume of *Handtooling for the Chunky Machine*, I give a shape for a basic yoked sweater. It is good to begin with this as it helps to understand the design of various styles, but first it is necessary to understand how raglan works.

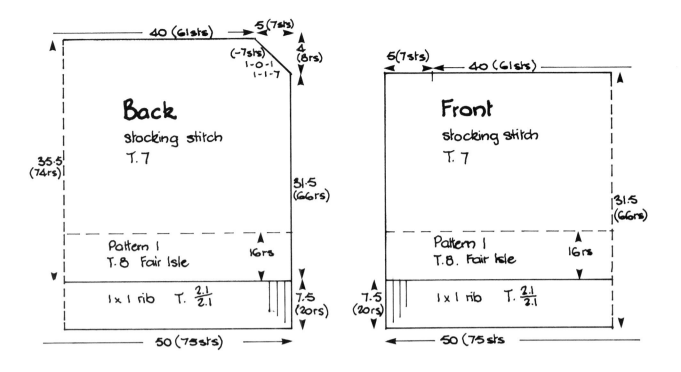

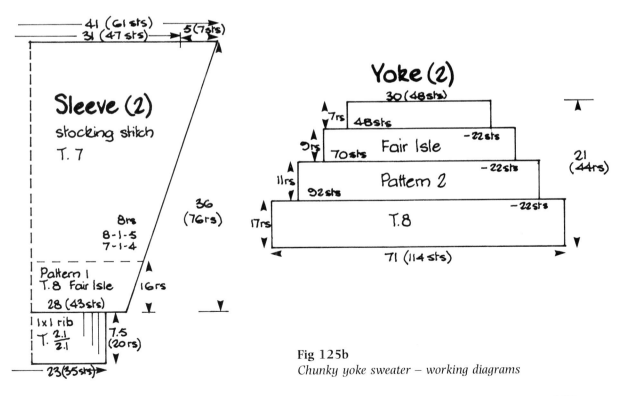

Fig 125b
Chunky yoke sweater – working diagrams

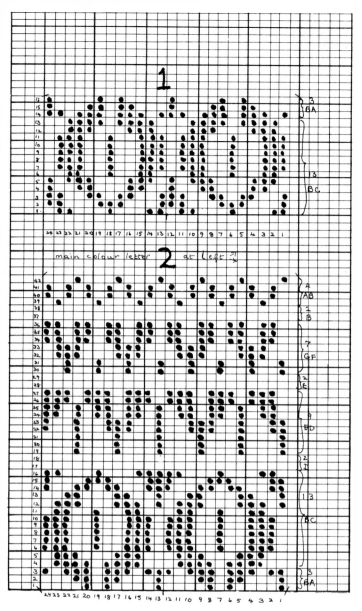

Fig 125c
Chunky yoke sweater – charts

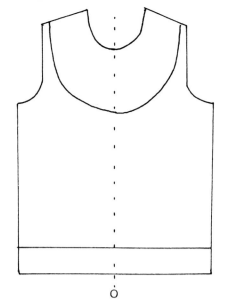

Fig 126 *(above)*
Sketch of a yoke on the fitted sleeve shape

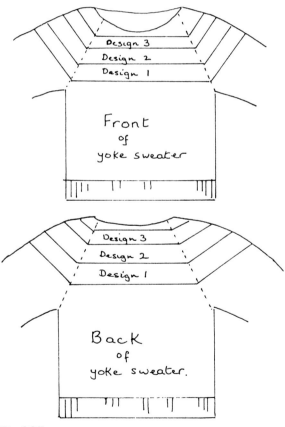

Fig 127
Yoke from the basic raglan

You could take the basic raglan shape from a branded pattern or from a sweater that fits you well. If you do either, check the armhole depth. On a classic raglan, the depth is usually a quarter of the body measurement. For yoked sweaters and chunky raglan tops I prefer the slightly looser shape provided by a quarter of the chest measurement plus a quarter total ease, usually around 5cm (2in) on a classic shape. If you have no raglan

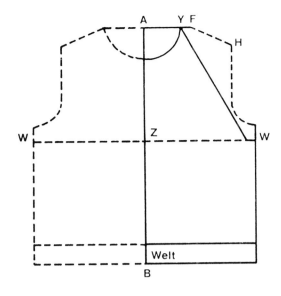

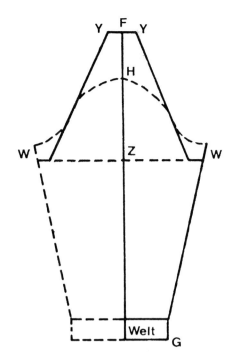

Fig 128
Constructing the raglan shape from the fitted sleeve block

shape, however, you can design your own. Please note, in this instance we are not dealing with the commercial raglan, which has extra cutout on the sleeve top.

When creating a raglan from the fitted sleeve block the main measurements remain unaltered, except for the following:

1. Line A–Z = $\frac{1}{4}$ of the bust/chest measurement plus ease.
2. Line A–F is the width of the back in the original. The line F–H is added to the sleeve head on the raglan, while $2 \times$ YF is the total measurement at the sleeve top (around 4–5cms [$1\frac{3}{4}$–2in]), the angle of the raglan diagonal at W being between 55–60°.
3. Re-draw front neck curve. Finish it within the raglan diagonal, leaving room for two stitches to be cast off at each neck edge at the front.
4. Make sure that the lines Y–W measure the same on back, front and sleeves.
5. Adjust underarm lengths. Take measurement from Z to bottom of the wrist, and not from W–G.

The Yoke on the basic raglan block

Draw and cut out the pieces separately. Cut the sleeve pieces in half vertically, four pieces altogether. Place the appropriate two with the back and the other two with the front. Put bits of adhesive underneath the pattern pieces to stop them moving. A kitchen table makes an ideal working base. Draw the yoke lines as shown. Note that the back is higher than the front and that though the lines are angular they will curve round in the knitting. There is no curved shaping on the front or on the back, but the yoke line on the back sleeve will have to drop towards the centre so that it can meet its counterpart from the front. All horizontal lines are measured and converted to stitches, and the measurement of the spaces between converted to rows according to pattern depth. The stitch differences between designs 1 and 3 are worked out as even distributions by the Magic Formula. The Japanese illustrate this part of the design as steps.

This particular shape is good as a starter. It works well with heavier yarns, and it does appear from time to time in Japanese patterns. In the finer

133

4-ply yarns, its major disadvantage becomes more apparent and that is that the stitches on the yoke are exactly the same as the number on the back, front and sleeves, and although the stitches can be picked up by hand knitters, or grafted stitch for stitch by machine knitters, the fact remains that the style does not allow for the same ease over the shoulders and the top as that allowed by the yoke shape with curved back and front, but that, as we shall see, has problems of its own.

As machine knitters knit full yokes in two sections: half sleeve, back, half sleeve, and half sleeve, front, half sleeve, two extra stitches are allowed for shoulder seaming, which is best done by mattress stitch or the figure-of-eight graft. Hand knitters who knit circular should take four stitches off the total complement. You will, of course, have to choose patterns that are suitable and you may have to juggle around with stitch quotas and make decisions regarding where the reductions will come. With seamless knitting, the pattern and not the designer always has the last word. When knitting the yoke in two pieces there will not be exact matches on the shoulder, but the joins need not be obtrusive if they are seamed invisibly.

Some years ago, I produced 18 sizes of quarter-scale raglan blocks with yoke lines marked for use in the charting device. I took the classic raglan shape as a jumping-off point. Then, spurred on by the Japanese expertise with yokes, I developed my own approach to design to teach to students in Further Education. The yoke and necklines were drawn with the help of a pair of compasses made from a stub of pencil connected to a drawing pin by a fine cord. The drawing pin was moved around the neckline in order to draw a parallel curve on the bottom part of the yoke. With a shallow yoke of course, I could indeed use a pair of compasses. All the pattern perimeter lines were then drawn within the yoke in the same way. Finally the yoke was cut

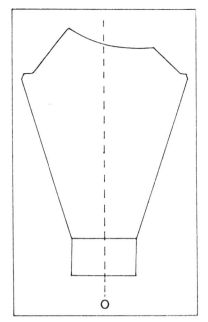

Fig 129
The opened out sleeve

away from all the pieces and when I opened out the sleeve I got the shape seen in the working diagrams on page 138. I could then draw all the diagrams for the main pieces on the charting device sheet. In a printed pattern, the Japanese represent the yoke breakdowns as steps so that one can see clearly how many stitches to reduce between patterns. As always, the Japanese leave the working out to the knitter and I follow suit.

The disadvantage of this modified style is that there are more stitches on the bottom edge of the yoke than there are on front, back and sleeves, and therefore there is a problem in grafting. The reason for the extra stitches is that the curves, which are

Fig 130
This curved stepped edge is created by short rows

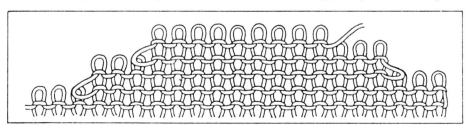

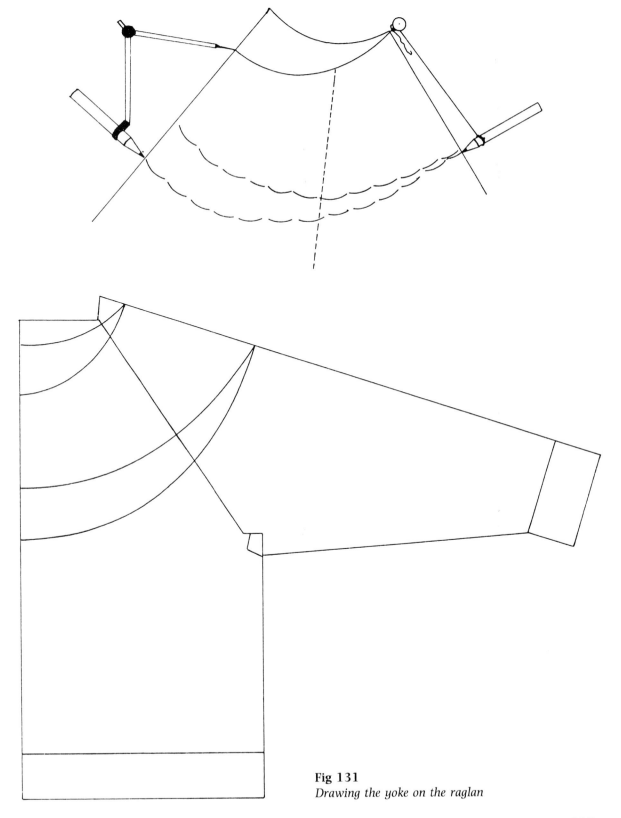

Fig 131
Drawing the yoke on the raglan

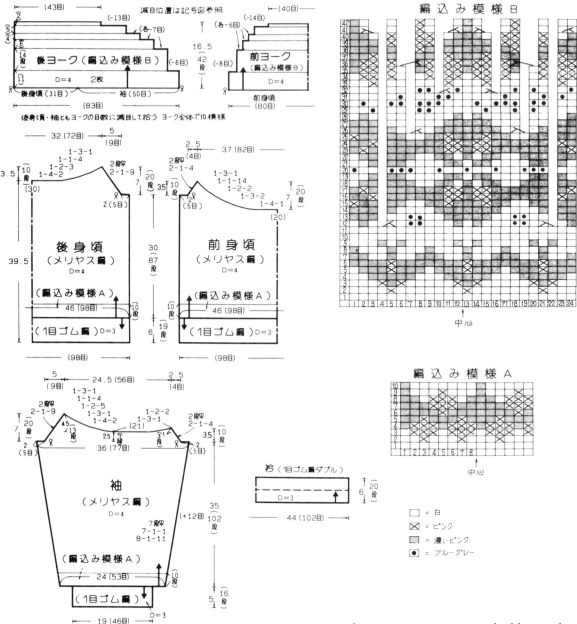

Fig 132

A Japanese pattern diagram for a machine-knitted yoked sweater. The Fair Isle pattern is hand-tooled and the five decrease sequences for the yoke are done in the popular hand-knitted way

rows on the main pieces, are matched by stitches on the yoke edge. Moreover, the tension gauge in Fair Isle produces more stitches per 10cm (4in). The extra stitches are grafted in to where there is most curve (Fig. 131). The advantages are that there is no pull down on the neck, the yoke is beautifully curved and fits like a dream. Any alteration to the shape of the neckline can be done

Fig 133
A sketched impression of the wife of Tuthankhamun wearing an ornamental yoke

by short rowing, and/or tension change after the knitting of the final pattern.

The style of yoke reminds me of the magnificent collars worn by the ancient Egyptian Pharaohs and their wives, collars which were often matched by heavy ornamentation at the wrists and hipline. Certainly the jewellery of ancient Egypt is one source of inspiration for my yoke design. Perhaps it is no coincidence that yoked sweaters often have bands of decoration above the cuffs and along the bottom edge to complement the main design around the neck. Moreover, designs viewed on the curve, like those on the bias, can make a refreshing change from those we view continually in horizontal or vertical bands.

The following pattern is a typical example of a raglan sweater with a full circular yoke.
Materials: 2/8s oiled Shetland. Total weight 284g. Approx 230g natural and small amounts in 13 additional colours.

Fig 134 *(below)*
Close-up of a machine-knitted yoked sweater featured in fig 135

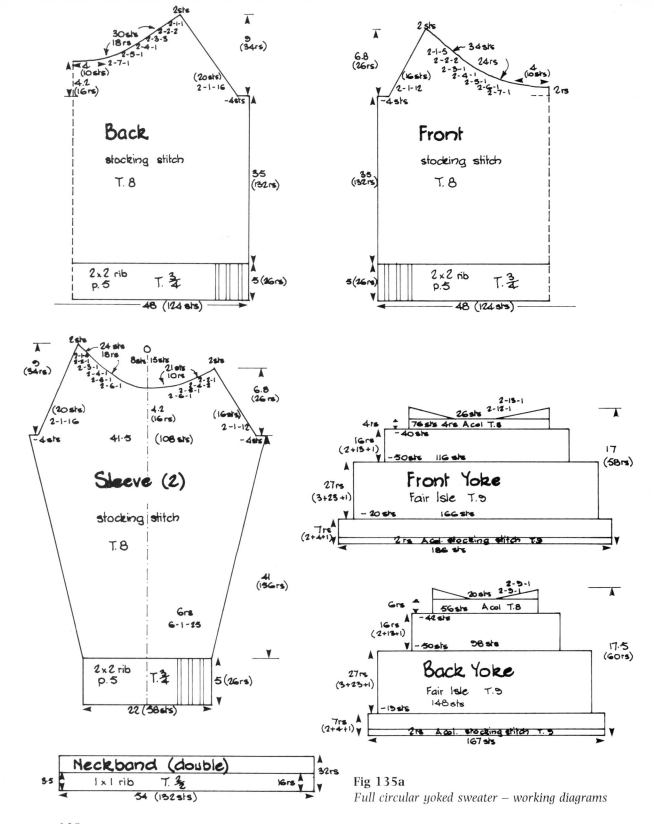

Fig 135a
Full circular yoked sweater – working diagrams

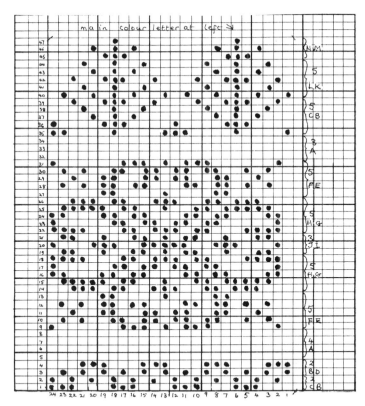

Fig 135b
Full circular yoked sweater – chart

Size: Bust 96cm (38in). Length 62cm (25in).
Sleeve length 50 cm (20in).

Machine: Standard punchcard or electronic
machine.

Needles: 2.75mm (US 2) needles for ribs, 3.25mm
(US 3) for stocking stitch and 3.75mm (US 5) for
Fair Isle.

Tension/gauge: Stocking stitch 26sts and 38rs per
10cm (4in); Fair Isle 27sts, 34rs per 10cm (4in)
when washed.

Directions:

1. Key: A natural (main), B bottle green, C pale
   hyacinth, D pale mint, E raspberry, F pale pink,
   G burgundy, H pale straw, I natural brown, J
   salmon pink, K moss green, L lovat green, M
   pale lime, N gooseberry lovat (14 colours).

2. ALL: Study pattern breakdowns carefully before

you knit. The yoke shapings on back, front and
sleeves are done in two half sections by means of
short rowing and then scrapping off separately
in WY. The second sleeve is knitted in reverse to
the first.

3. Yoke (2 pieces): add 2 sts (not counted) for the
   seam. Begin with WY. Mark centre stitch. Note
   stocking stitch rows on each side of the pattern.
   The decreasing is done in the single row at the
   end of the pattern (see the Chunky Circular-
   yoked Sweater on page 130).

4. Neck shaping is done by the short row method,
   first on one side and then on the other.

5. MK: Graft the extra stitches on the yoke to the
   loops on the short row curves. HK: To knit the
   yoke pieces pick up the loops and stitches below
   WY.

Fig 135c
Full circular yoked sweater

TEN

Bias knitting

I define bias knitting as that which follows an angle to the horizontal of around 45 degrees, sometimes more, sometimes less, but never 90 degrees, *i.e.* perpendicular, which is the conventional way, or 180 degrees for sideways knitting. Geometric intarsias can follow bias principles even though they are surface patterns and have nothing to do with structure. Perhaps the most interesting area of bias knitting is the all-in-one garment where the knitted structure eases the surface pattern into automatic V-shaped or inverted chevrons.

There is some bias knitting to do on virtually every garment one tackles, unless one is content to stay with the simple T-shape of four rectangles and a slit neck: an example can be seen in the sleeve seam with its underarm increases or decreases.

Although bias knitting of one form or another has been done for some considerable time, there is no record of how the knitter arrived at the breakdowns, and one is forced to the conclusion that he/she could not explain in mathematical terms. The designer of the stocking-stitch repair

Fig 136
Conventional, sideways and bias-knitted shapes

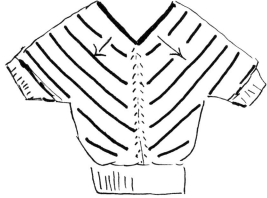

Fig 137
Drawing of a hand-knitted top with integral chevron shaping

patch in *Mrs Leach's Fancy Work-Basket* (1886) no doubt produced it after much trial and error, and she certainly knew how to use paired increases and decreases on the sides of the integrally knitted diamond. She must have had real faith in her readers' ability to adapt. Most knitters today would have to have it in black and white. 'After one piece

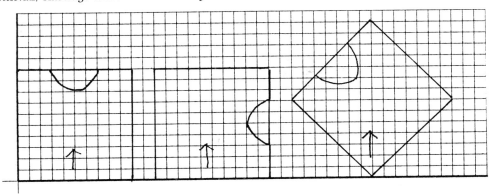

Fig 138
*Nineteenth-century bias-knitted garter stitch mat
and quilt piece*

has been worked, it can easily be seen where to
make it larger, in case it does not cover the place
that needs repairing.'

When it came to DIY garments, it would have
been a case of knitting out one's idea and placing
the result against a paper pattern as did Flora
Klickman. Alterations and shaping would then
have been made until the right measurements
were achieved. Equally, today, there are hand
knitters who fiercely defend the experimental
approach, and who refuse any advice from machine knitters. They are right to defend what they
enjoy, and who are we to deny them? However, a
machine knitter's response is that one's energy and
time could be saved for widening the design scope
and that understanding is a great aid to enjoyment.
Indeed, one's creativity is crippled by non-compre-
hension. The choice before us is rather like prefer-
ring the pigeon post to the telephone.

Bias Knitting in the 1930s

During the 1930s, there was great interest in bias
knitting. Although none of the great knitting

authorities discussed the principles in manuals,
bias knitting in both garter and stocking stitch
appeared in a lot of patterns. It is interesting that in
quite a few of these patterns, both the stitch and the
row tensions are given. Did the designer/pattern-
writer understand what could not be communi-

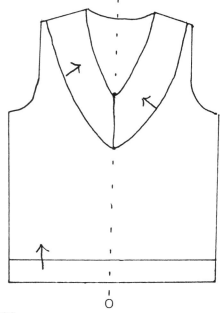

Fig 139
Drawing to show a V-yoke

in the pattern; instead, the written instructions are two full columns long.

Two of the most beautiful patterns I can find incorporating knitting on the bias are a jumper and skirt in *Woman and Home* (1934). Each garment is knitted in stocking stitch, with paired increases and decreases which create a chevron. To correct the shape for the neckline, stitches are picked up at the top 'V' and a triangle is graft-knitted in the conventional way. The sleeves are worked similarly. There are no charts and there are pages and pages of instructions.

Similarly, Catherine Frank's *The Pictorial Guide to Modern Home Knitting* (1939), is full of large, clear, black and white photographs, probably the best I've seen from the 1930s. She has photographs of samples to illustrate decreasing and increasing, processes which of course create bias edges, but her explanations are infuriatingly vague: 'Knitted fabric is made narrower by decreasing the number of stitches, and it is made wider by increasing the number of stitches. Both these processes are simple, but as each has several variations, the right one must be used.' She does not tell us how to find the right one. It is up to the knitter to choose 'the best one suited to her purpose'.

Garter stitch on the bias

The Victorians knew how to bias knit using garter stitch. There are some examples of quilt squares knitted corner to corner in *Mrs Leach's Fancy Work-Basket* and Richard Rutt writes of the women in the Shaker community in the USA. They used to knit circular cloths in garter stitch, employing radial short rows. The modern American garter stitch afghan, it seems, has a history of at least 100 years.

Since garter stitch is simply knit stitch on every row, it is tempting to think that it came before stocking stitch, In fact, garter stitch is knit stitch worked on two needles, while stocking stitch was originally circular knit stitch on four or five needles. Flat knit stitch with two needles, *i.e.* garter stitch, came after circular knitting with four or five needles. Stocking stitch, *i.e.* one row knit, one row purl on two needles, was even more recent. In her book *The Pictorial Guide to Modern Home Knitting*, Catherine Franks features two interesting little

Fig 140
Dress worked in knitweave and tuck with a deep V-yoke (Lois Franklin, 1982)

cated for commercial reasons? If so, then the understanding died with her.

In an issue of *Modern Home* (1933), there is a pattern for a wool front, like a dickey, to wear with an autumn suit. Though this article is knitted conventionally in stocking stitch, it incorporates a striking two-coloured, diagonal intarsia design which requires on the part of the designer, an understanding of bias principles. The tension is $7\frac{1}{2}$ stitches and 9 rows to 1in (2.5cm), and the indications are that the pattern should be charted out on mini-gridded graph paper. No chart is given

Fig 141
All-in-one integrally machine-knitted raglan

samples in garter stitch. Both are bias knitted. One is a trapezoid/parallelogram and the other a right-angled triangle. She decreases/increases one stitch every row, or decreases/increases one stitch every other row, but she does not give the reasons for her choice.

It is interesting that when Flora Klickman incorporated bias knitted sections into her garment patterns she chose garter stitch. There is even a cape attached to a hood in her *Modern Knitting* (1916), which has chevrons shaped by paired decreases. Certainly, garter stitch was a popular choice for patterns during the 1930s and early 1940s for bias knitting. No one until today, however, had attempted to explain in mathematical terms why garter stitch is nearly always

chosen by hand knitters for bias knitting, and why stocking stitch is avoided by all except the most expert. One practical reason is that garter stitch always lies flat. That garter stitch usually has a gauge of 1:2 has been common knowledge for a long time, but only recently has it been understood that an application of the Magic Formula makes it easy to bias knit in patterns other than garter stitch.

American handknitters and garter stitch

I have been kindly sent from the USA a copy of *Number Knitting: The New All-Way-stretch Method* by Virginia Woods Bellamy, (1952, Crown). Interestingly, there is only one technique in this book and that concerns units of bias knitting in garter stitch. The edge of one unit is picked up and another unit is knitted from that. On the advice of

Elizabeth Blondell, editor of *McCalls Needlework* magazine, who was convinced that here was 'a new idea in knitting', Virginia Woods Bellamy patented her discovery. Her lawyer advised her that the units of number knitting were two, the square and the triangle. When there is evidence of earlier hand knitters doing bias knitted squares and triangles, incorporating similar techniques, it is puzzling that a patent application was even considered.

In *Modern Needlecraft* (1932), Marjory Tillotson shows how to pick up and knit from the edge loops of a piece of garter stitch knitting, but there are possibly two features in the approach of Virginia Woods Bellamy which are at least highly individual if not original.

1. She makes her fabrics by knitting in units, *i.e.* squares, triangles and rectangles, picked up from one another. Corners are frequently turned by short rowing. The fabric will stretch in any direction and even though it is knitted more loosely than most knit fabrics, it will always spring back to its original form.

2. She has her own symbol system, and works entirely by chart on square-gridded graph paper. This is correct for garter stitch if you take the height of the mini-grid to equal two rows, and two rows, to Virginia Woods Bellamy, is a ridge.

It is rather strange that very few people have ever heard of this lady and even fewer attempt her pick-up technique today. The short-row methods that are seen in the work of Elizabeth Zimmerman, and in various issues of *Knitters* magazine, are much more popular because the fabric is more efficiently knitted and shaped. Moreover, Virginia Woods Bellamy does not seem to know how to knit short rows sideways to produce a square.

Since Virginia Woods Bellamy's technique is patented in her book *Number Knitting*, I gladly recommend the Japanese method of charting bias knitting sections in garter stitch. Nevertheless, Virginia Woods Bellamy's book is good to read because she conveys the excitement of discovery. She directed herself to knit a square:

'12 stitches × 12 ridges – cast off. Turn sideways and pick up the 12 edge stitches –

another 12 ridges knitted on those 12 stitches . . . Excited by the establishment of a mathematical square I went further. If I could decrease at the edge of each ridge by just one stitch, would I not come to one stitch at the end of 12 ridges, and have a triangle? I tried it. I had a triangle.'

A little over 36 years later, we may smile, but such enthusiastic writing is delightful to read, and what is more, there are some very attractive garments as a result.

Elizabeth Zimmerman and garter stitch

If Virginia Woods Bellamy laid the foundation of the American enthusiasm for bias knitted garter stitch, then Elizabeth Zimmerman certainly developed it. In her *Knitting Workshop* (1981), there is a most interesting chapter 'Great Garter Stitch', and some original and beautiful garments to knit based on bias knitting in garter stitch. In the hands of Elizabeth Zimmerman, garter stitch fabric is shaped and curved so that there are few seams, and there is certainly no need to pick up edges to give crossways stretch. To encourage the timid, Elizabeth Zimmerman emphasizes how little understanding of maths is required. Indeed, the maths is simple. Working on the basis of one stitch every other row for garter stitch, shapes are easily planned on graph paper. Elizabeth Zimmerman, however, does not move on to bias-knit in other stitch patterns and neither, it seems, do her devotees. It is significant that in issues of *Knitters* magazine the hand knitters stay with garter stitch and the machine knitters move to stocking stitch, inviting the hand knitters to follow suit. After all, garter stitch has disadvantages. It is stiff and dense, and can have a corrugated appearance when worn. It is also slow to accomplish.

In *Knitters* Issue 5, there is an intriguing garter stitch rib warmer (shorty sleeveless waistcoat) by Elizabeth Zimmerman, knitted virtually seamless. The garment incorporates bias knitting to curve the corners on the back round to the front and vice versa. Beside it, and with Elizabeth Zimmerman's permission, is a stocking stitch version designed by Susanna Lewis and with the short row breakdowns

Fig 143a and b
Photograph showing bias-knitted squares worked in knitweave, stocking and garter stitches and diagram showing breakdowns for a stocking stitch square

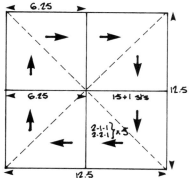

worked out by the Magic Formula. In *A Machine Knitter's Guide to Creating Fabrics*, Susanna Lewis illustrates a perfect square, sideways knitted in stocking stitch with its angles dissected into two of 45 degrees each. Many hand knitters believe that you can only do this kind of knitting in garter stitch and this is why there is such reluctance to go beyond it.

In my little hand-knit stocking stitch sample, I had a stitch and row gauge of 24sts and 31rs per 10cm (4in) with 4mm needles. Even without the

Magic Formula, I could see in a flash that the ratio was near enough 3:4. Therefore in 4rs there were 3sts to be short-rowed. Since we work in pairs of rows, the sum would be 2sts one row and 1 stitch the next, *i.e.* alternate, row. If I had used a fancy bouclé yarn, I would have got a very different stitch and row gauge. Certainly I had a problem when I came to doing the square sample in knitweave, with a gauge of 23sts and 54rs. There was only one foolproof method to use and that was the Magic Formula.

The Magic Formula: Expression 3
(see Chapter 4 for expressions 1 and 2)

In this expression of the Magic Formula, the stitches are the ones to be held in short rowing every alternate row. They are not decreased or

Fig 142
The Bond machine. The extension is used for lengthy bias pieces

increased. Even though it can be seen immediately what the breakdowns are in the gauge of 24sts and 31rs in stocking stitch, it does provide a good example of Magic Formula use which can be applied in more difficult situations.

In this example I drew a sketch of the square and wrote on the measurements, but it is best to draw other polygons within a circle. Take the perimeter of the shape to be same as the circumference, the measurement of which is achieved by the sum 2piR. Any slight difference in measurement between the circumference and perimeter is evened out in the working. One must add 1 stitch, occasionally 2, to remain constant in the working. In this example, $2.4 \times 6.25 = 15$. I added 1 (see chapter 4) making 16sts to cast on over a WY crochet cord of 17 chains. Begin with a purl row.

Fig 144
Sideways knitted polygon worked on a chunky machine

Please note that here I am dealing with a mini-square, which is one of four sub-divided into two right-angled triangles. The breakdowns are the same for each triangle, but the second lot are mirrored in reverse to the first. They are worked every other knit row, mitre fashion for the first half, where most stitches are knitted first, and then reduced to one. For the second half, the breakdowns are worked flare fashion, where the least are knitted first, working towards the most. The Magic Formula sum, which in this instance we don't really need to do, is:

$$\begin{array}{c} 1+1 \\ 10\ \big/\overline{15} \\ \underline{5}\quad \underline{10} \\ 5\qquad 5 \end{array}$$

I add 1 to be the constant (see chapter 4), making 16 altogether. I have written the breakdowns on the diagram in the economical Japanese way. I used the lacy method of short rowing and slipped the first stitch after the gap on the purl row. On completion, the open edges were grafted together and the WY removed.

In modern British hand-knit literature, there are remarkably few garments which incorporate bias knitting in any significant way although the work of Maggie Whiting provides one notable exception. There are, however, more bias knitted garments in German hand-knit publications than in any other publications I have seen in the West, and these

Fig 145
Bias-knitted garment shapes

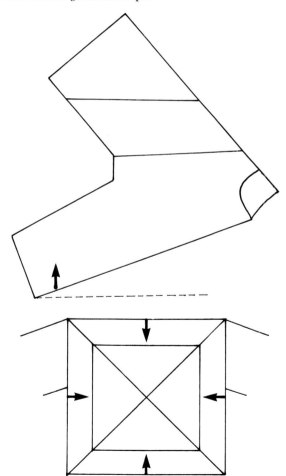

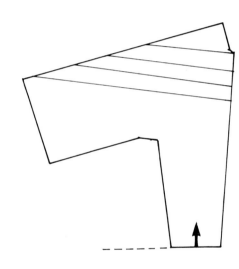

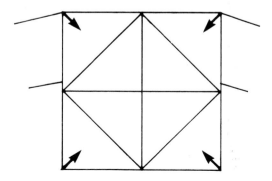

garments are by no means confined to garter stitch. Even machine knitters outside Japan do not seem to be very interested in bias knitting, although patterns do appear from time to time which feature large sections. One way to begin is to incorporate a deep V insertion in a top. There is a magnificent example in Fair Isle in *Brother Fashion* (Vol. 13), while in Rowan's *Summer and Winter* knitting there is a photograph of Carrie White's beautiful machine-knit jacket which has a similar deep V collar-cum-yoke. Carrie White and Maggie Whiting are two designers who, I feel, understand the relationship between surface pattern and garment structure.

One thing is sure: bias knitting is not a good choice for a pattern writer who has to produce a design in six sizes. If you have no means to communicate with economy and clarity, then it is best to leave bias knitting alone. In my view, the Japanese have the most suitable communicating vehicle of any knitting tradition. I have yet to see in English a clear explanation of how pattern breakdowns have been achieved in bias and chevron knitting.

Illustrated opposite are some garment sketches to show the use of bias knitting. The arrows in the diagrams indicate the direction of knitting. In all bias knitting, look for a right-angled triangle; it may be hidden or it may be apparent, and there may be more than one. If it is hidden, then dot in the missing lines. Translate the measurements of the horizontal and vertical sections into stitches and rows, whichever applies, and work out the breakdowns along the hypotenuse edge with the aid of the Magic Formula. Balance out the breakdowns as evenly as possible and see that they match those on a corresponding diagonal to achieve the same angle of rise. For example, the diagonals on a raglan sleeve head should match those on the back and front, even though the breakdowns may not be identical. Machine knitters can use a charting device, but watch when you get to a corner, that the sheet does not direct you to cast off and cast on again immediately. It is wise to be a little ahead of the charter.

Some breakdowns are best planned on every other row. Others will be paired increases and decreases, as on a long sleeve. You must decide whether the shapings come at each end of one row or at the beginning of the next two rows. An isosceles triangle which has two identical diagonals, *i.e.* a double dart or flare, will be divided into two right-angled triangles, *i.e.* one dart or half a flare. The breakdowns will be worked out for one of them and will apply to both, *i.e.* the complete isosceles triangle, as paired shapings. If the shape is knitted sideways, the breakdowns for the second half will work in reverse. For a square, knitted corner to corner, there will be increases to the centre diagonal, and then decreases to balance. Quite often in bias knitting there are increases to large amounts of stitches. A machine knitter should check whether there are sufficient needles. If not, then the garment should be re-designed or tuck stitch mosaics substituted for Fair Isle.

Some garments which have bias knitted sections on just the back and front can be worked out on a sketch diagram. Hand knitters will be able to knit the front composed of four squares and the one with four triangles integrally with paired increases or decreases at the centre of their knitting. Please remember that to get the shape, you need to work out the breakdowns correctly. It is no good 'just trying' decreasing every other row or increasing every fourth row. This experimental approach is, I know, a hand-knit tradition, and it is quite often described as 'being creative', but the method is a bad one for this kind of knitting, and an enormous and frustrating time waster. Moreover, 'just trying' reveals a lack of understanding of the principles involved.

The more complex, all-in-one garments, where the bias knitting automatically produces V or inverted-V shaped chevrons, need to be drafted very carefully. When the measurements of a right-angled triangle are involved, you can get away with a sketch and the application of the Pythagorean theorem – the square on the hypotenuse equals the sum of the squares on the other two sides. It may, however, be reassuring to draft for the first time. If you have no charting device, cut out the piece full scale on plain white paper. Even newspaper is alright if you have the appropriate tools to give you correct angles. Put the paper pattern on a table with white paper underneath. Make sure that the pattern is tilted at around 45° to the horizontal and then secure with pieces of adhesive underneath. Study the pattern very carefully for the hidden right-angled triangles, which will give the Magic Formula breakdowns for shaping along the bias edges. In some cases, for example the two designs (see Fig 145) which stand on their sleeve corner and bottom edge, the invisible triangles are best drawn outside some parts of the outline. In this case, draw them on to the white paper underneath. You may well have different shapings to work out on each side of the sleeve. Keep the neck shaping very simple on all bias knitting.

When you are satisfied that you have drawn in

all the triangles for shaping purposes, transfer the drawings as sketches to your notebook. Then measure all the relevant lines, including those for the invisible triangles. Transfer all information to your notebook. Work out the stitch and row breakdowns with your calculator and the Magic Formula. Re-arrange the breakdowns so that you can follow them easily.

Study the mohair top with bias knitted stripes. It is a good idea to draw a second sketch on which to write the breakdowns, using the Japanese format for ease of following. The original drawing can be used again and again as the basis for any stitch pattern and gauge of your choice. The breakdowns will be different in each case but that does not matter if all else is correct. The knitted shape will then be an identikit copy of the paper pattern. Charting device users may copy the paper pattern

Fig 146
Student in a Japanese knitting school blocking and pressing knitwear

straight on to the sheet. In some cases, they only need to copy half.

All this of course, sounds much more complicated than it really is. Once you have a paper pattern cut-out, the whole exercise becomes an easy and absorbing activity. There is an inbuilt resistance in the minds of many hand and machine knitters to starting off with a paper pattern, and we need to overcome our inhibitions if we want to do any truly adventurous knitting. If the shape is complex, the surface pattern need not be. Horizontal bands of colour, texture and/or lace produce the most intriguing diagonals, chevrons, squares and diamonds in bias knitting.

In Fig 145, the two designs standing on their sleeve ends will have to be knitted in reverse for the second half. There will be four pieces, a pair each with identical shapings. Seam the pieces very carefully up the centre. They can be crocheted together or you can graft knit the first piece into the second as the knitting proceeds. All cuffs and welts are added on completion. In garments where only the back and front are bias knitted, thought needs to be given to the kind of sleeves one ought to have. Consider my choice for the following mohair top pattern and note the broken lines of stripes.

Bias-knitted Mohair Top

Materials: Mohair. 200g French navy, 75g red, 50g each pink, grey, pale blue.
Size: Bust 100cm (40in). Length 59cm (23½in). Sleeve length 49cm (19½in).
Machine: Brother 260 chunky and intarsia carriage.
Needles: use 4.5mm (US 7) for ribs and 5.5mm (US 9) for stocking stitch.
Tension/gauge: 16sts and 20rs per 10cm (4in) over striped stocking stitch pattern and intarsia sleeves.
Directions:

1. Key: **R** red, **B** pale blue, **G** grey, **P** pink, **N** French navy.
2. Colour sequences of stripes: on back/front triangles, starting from WY in the centre: 1r N, * 4rs R, 2rs N, 4rs P, 2rs N, 4rs B, 2rs N, 4rs G, 2rs N. Repeat from * to end (2sts).
3. Note. Bottom edge is a hem. Knit a cord, 1r knit, 1r slip, over 4sts, if required.

Bias knitting is also good for cut-and-sew. Some

Fig 147a
Bias-knitted top worked in mohair

shapes of course, require considerably more material and have therefore more wastage than others.

The use of graph paper

You can choose to map out the whole of your bias knitted garment on to stitch-related graph paper. For bias knitting, however, the ratio of the grid to the stitch and row gauge must be as near correct as possible as you will find it difficult to get away with distortion in bias knitting if you have used the wrong grid of graph paper. The next stage is to step out the shapings. This at first may seem easier than adopting the Japanese approach, but then you have to group the shaping breakdowns into manageable working order to follow in your knitting. In other words, you have taken a circuitous route to achieve the breakdowns the Magic Formula will give you in a flash. The choice, as always, is yours.

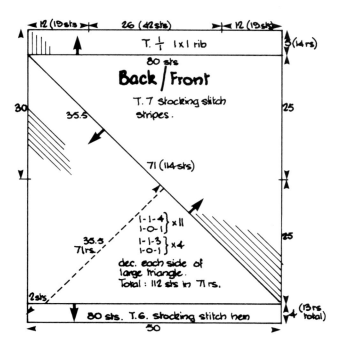

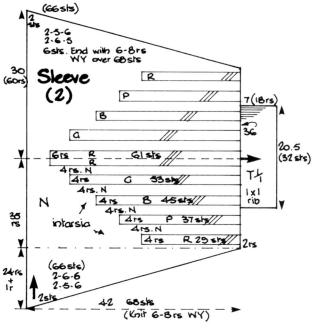

Fig 147b
Bias-knitted top – working diagrams

Pattern inspiration for bias knitting

Since triangles and chevrons often form an integral part of bias knitted garments, they direct our attention to consider primitive garment shapes like plaids, shawls and ponchos. I also found I was looking for inspiration to ancient Greek and Roman pavements, to early medieval illuminated manuscripts and to Oriental and Middle Eastern carpets, where the design changes direction as soon as it comes to a corner. Bias knitted garments also provide plenty of scope for pattern contrast. The chevron shaped section can be the more dramatic with a subdued background pattern throwing it into relief, or the opposite can prevail.

Postscript

Working for this book, then, has provided me with a rare insight into a doubly rich craft world. It has been possible as never before to pull together a little from the wealth of two knitting cultures which spring out of the British tradition. The majority of knitters will, however, state their preference for hand or machine, at least for the time being. I trust that there will be less reticence about looking over the wall to see what can be learned and gathered from the other side. Where there has been silence there can now be communication and an age-old antagonism will finally be laid to rest.

ADDITIONAL REFERENCES

Chapter 1
William Lee, 'Quatercentenary Publication',
Knitting International, Leicester, 1989
Marilyn Palmer, *Framework Knitting*, Shire,
1984

Chapter 2
Brayshaw & Robinson, *The History of the Ancient
Parish of Giggleswick*, Halton, London, 1932
Ken Etherege, *Welsh Costume in the Eighteenth
and Nineteenth Centuries*, Christopher Davies,
Swansea, 1977
Hartley & Ingilby, *The Old Handknitters of the
Dales*, Dalesman, 1951
Markrich & Kiewe, *Victorian Fancy-work*, Pitman,
1975
Geoffrey Warner, *A Stitch in Time: Victorian and
Edwardian Needlecraft*, David & Charles, 1975
Mary Wright, *Cornish Guernseys and Knit-frocks*,
Hodge-Ethnographica, 1979

Chapter 3
Kiewe, *Sacred History of Knitting*, ANI, Oxford,
1970
Kathleen Kinder, *Second Resource Book for
Machine Knitters*, Kinder, 1980
Jane Rapley, 'Handframe Knitting: the
development of patterning and shaping',
Textile History 6
Michael Harvey, *Patons: A Story of Handknitting*,
Springwood Books, 1985

Chapter 5
Helen Bennett, *Scottish Knitting*, Shire, 1986

Chapter 6
Frances Hinchcliffe, *Knit one, Purl One – Historic
and Contemporary Knitting from the Victoria and
Albert's Collection*, 1985

Chapter 7
John Allen, *The Machine Knitting Book*, Dorling
Kindersley, 1985
Kaffe Fassett, *Glorious Knitting*, Century, 1985
Kaffe Fassett, *Kaffe Fassett at the V & A*, Guild
Publishing, 1988
Felicity Murray, *Design Your Own Machine
Knitwear*, Foulsham, 1985
Linda Parry, *William Morris Textiles*, Weidenfeld
& Nicholson, 1983
Richard Thames, *William Morris*, Shire, 1972
Sally Ann Elliott, *Creative Machine Knitting*,
Windward-Frances Hodge 1988

Chapter 9
Vogue Knitting: Autumn-Winter 1985,
Bohus Knitting

Chapter 10
Jane Waller (ed), *A Stitch in Time: Knitting and
Crochet Patterns of the 1920s, 30s and 40s*,
Duckworth, 1972
Knitters' Magazine, PO Box 1525, Sioux Falls,
SD57101, USA
Anne L. MacDonald, *No Idle Hands: The Social
History of American Knitting*, Ballantine Books,
New York, 1988

BOOKS OF TECHNIQUES

Hand knitting

The Illustrated Dictionary of Knitting Rae Compton (Batsford, 1988).

The Encyclopaedia of Knitting Techniques Debbie Robinson (Michael Joseph, 1986)

Knitting Your Own Designs for a Perfect Fit (1982) and *The Handknitters Handbook* Montse Stanley (David and Charles, 1986).

Mary Thomas' Knitting Book (Dover reprint, 1985).

Machine Knitting

The Machine Knitters Dictionary Linda Gartshore (Batsford, 1983).

Techniques in Machine Knitting Kathleen Kinder (Batsford, 1983).

Handtooling for the Chunky Knitting Machine (2 vols) (Kathleen Kinder, 1987/8).

An Illustrated Handbook of Machine Knitting Janet Nabney (Batsford, 1987).

Machine Knitting Technology Mary Weaver (Mary Weaver, 1980).

Guild Addresses

The Knitting Guild of America,
PO Box 166,
Knoxville,
Tennessee, 37901.

The Edinburgh Knitting and Crochet Guild,
c/o 9 Lennie Cottages,
Craigs Road,
Edinburgh, EH12 0BB.

The Knitting and Crochet Guild,
c/o 5 Roman Mount,
Roundhay,
Leeds LS8 2DP.

USEFUL ADDRESSES

Book Suppliers (HK)
Bayswater Books,
21 Gwendolen Ave,
London SW15 6ET.

Crafts of Quality Books, (MK also)
49 Gelston Point,
Burwell Close,
London E1 2NR.

The Design Centre Bookshop,
28 Haymarket,
London SW1Y 4SU.

Fibrecrafts,
Style Cottage,
Lower Eashing,
Godalming,
Surrey GU7 2QP.

Ries Wools, (yarns also)
242 High Holborn,
London WC1.

The Textile Bookshop,
Tynwald Mills,
St Johns,
IOM.

Books and Supplies (MK)
BSK Ltd,
Murdock Road,
Manton Industrial Estate,
Bedford MK41 7LE.

Computaknit,
31 Market Place,
Kendal,
Cumbria.

Knitcraft,
131 High St,
Yiewsley,
West Drayton,
Middlesex UB7 7HZ.

Knitmates,
28 Church St,
Ifield Road,
West Green,
Crawley,
West Sussex RH11 7BG.

The Knitting Neuk, (importer Nihon Vogue MK
magazines)
32 Ashley Road,
Aberdeen.

Metropolitan,
The Pinfold,
Poole,
nr. Nantwich,
Cheshire CW5 6AL.

Nihon Vogue Ltd (H & MK)
34 Ichigaya-Honmuracho,
Shinjuku-Ku,
Tokyo 162.

Yarn and Supplies (HK)
Dyed in the Wool, (H & MK)
The Sidings,
Settle,
N. Yorkshire.

Patons and Baldwins,
Darlington,
Co. Durham.

Creativity, (H & MK)
26 New Oxford St,
London WC1.

Colour Way, (H & MK)
112A Westbourne Grove,
London W2 5RU.

Rowan Yarns, (H & MK)
Green Lane Mill,
Washpit,
Holmfirth,
W. Yorkshire.

Twentieth Century Yarns Ltd, (H & MK)
The Red House,
Guilsborough,
Northants NN6 8PU.

Yarns and Supplies (MK)
Readicut Wool Co.,
Terry Mills,
Ossett,
Wakefield WF5 9SA.

Bramwell Yarns,
Unit 5,
Metcalf Drive,
Altham Lane,
Accrington,
Lancs BB5 5TU.

Brockwell Wools,
Stansfield Mill,
Triangle,
W. Yorkshire HX6 3LZ.

T. Forsell and Sons Ltd,
Blaby Road,
South Wigston,
Leicester LE8 2SG.

Yarnarama,
240/50 Lowerhouse Lane,
Burnley.

Yarn Markets UK,
North Street East,
Uppingham,
Leicester LE15 9QT.

USA: yarns and supplies
HK
Fiber Works,
313 East 45th St.
NY 10017.

School House Press, (books also)
6899 Carey Bluff,
Pittsville,
WI 54466.

Straw into Gold, (books also)
3006 San Pablo Ave,
Berkeley,
CA.

Tomato Factory Yarn Co.,
31 Railroad Place,
Hopewell,
NJ 08525.

Westminster Trading, (books also)
5 Northern Boulevard,
Amherst,
NH 03031.

The Yarn Barn,
918 Massachusetts,
PO Box 334,
Lawrence,
Kansas 66044.

MK (yarns and books)
Chameleon,
617 Massachusetts Ave,
Indianapolis,
IN.

The Knitting Machine Centre,
5442 Cannas Drive,
Cincinatti,
Ohio 45238.

Frances Collins Importer,
PO Box 8244,
Midland,
Texas 79708.

Kruh Knits,
PO Box 1587,
Farmington Valley Arts Center,
Avon Park North,
Avon
CT 06001.

Betty's Knit Shop,
4020 Lambert Road,
E1 Sobrante,
CA 94803.

Fran's Knitting Boutique,
651 Main Street,
Patuxent Place,
Laurel,
Maryland 20707.

Index